BIO
Der

Deraniyagala,
  Sonali.

Wave.

$24.00

DATE			
14c 6/16			
12c 10/14 , 2/16			

3/13

D0065821

Goshen Public Library
366 Main Street
Goshen, NY 10924

BAKER & TAYLOR

Wave

SONALI DERANIYAGALA

Goshen Public Library
366 Main Street
Goshen, NY 10924

ALFRED A. KNOPF · NEW YORK 2013

THIS IS A BORZOI BOOK
PUBLISHED BY ALFRED A. KNOPF

Copyright © 2013 by Sonali Deraniyagala

All rights reserved. Published in the United States by Alfred A.
Knopf, a division of Random House, Inc., New York, and in
Canada by McClelland & Stewart Limited, an imprint of
Random House of Canada, Limited, Toronto.

www.aaknopf.com

Knopf, Borzoi Books, and the colophon are registered
trademarks of Random House, Inc.

Grateful acknowledgment is made to Alfred Publishing for
permission to reprint an excerpt from "There Is a Light That
Never Goes Out," by Steven Morrissey and Johnny Marr.
Copyright © 1987 Artemis Muziekuitgeverij B.V. (BUM/STE)
and Universal Music Publishing Limited (GB) (PRS). All Rights
on Behalf of Artemis Muziekuitgeverij B.V. administered by
Warner-Tamerlane Publishing Corp. Reprinted by permission
of Alfred Publishing. All Rights Reserved.

LIBRARY OF CONGRESS CATALOGING-IN-PUBLICATION DATA
Deraniyagala, Sonali.
Wave / Sonali Deraniyagala.
p.   cm.
"Borzoi Books."
ISBN 978-0-307-96269-0
1. Deraniyagala, Sonali.   2. Deraniyagala,
Sonali—Family.   3. Disaster victims—Sri Lanka—
Biography.   4. Widows—Biography.   5. Indian
Ocean Tsunami, 2004.   6. Bereavement.   7. Parents—
Death.   8. Children—Death.   I. Title.
CT1528.D47A3 2013
954.9303'2092—dc23   [B]   2012040980

Jacket design by Carol Devine Carson

Manufactured in the United States of America

First Edition

To Alexandra and Kristiana

One

I thought nothing of it at first. The ocean looked a little closer to our hotel than usual. That was all. A white foamy wave had climbed all the way up to the rim of sand where the beach fell abruptly down to the sea. You never saw water on that stretch of sand. It was our friend Orlantha who alerted me. A short while before, she'd knocked on our door to ask if we were ready to leave. We almost were. Steve was in the shower, or reading on the toilet more likely. Our two boys were on the back veranda, buzzing around their Christmas presents.

This was Yala, a national park on the southeastern coast of Sri Lanka. White-bellied sea eagles abound here, and for Vikram they were the most splendid of birds. For a nearly eight-year-old, Vikram knew heaps about birds. A pair of sea eagles nested near the lagoon that edged this hotel in Yala, and he'd sit on a rock on the lagoon's shore and wait hours, hungry for a glimpse of them. They always turned up, as reliable as the tooth fairy.

We had spent four days here, with my parents.

Wave

In less than a week Steve, the boys, and I would be flying home to London. We had driven down to Yala from Colombo on the morning after Malli's violin concert. Not that Malli had any commitment to the violin, it was being onstage he loved. He stood there and mimicked the little girl next to him, flourishing his bow with convincing exactness. "He's faking it, Mum, he's faking it," Vik whispered to me that night at the concert, impressed by his five-year-old brother's brazen nerve.

Our friend Orlantha gave Malli violin lessons on our trips to Sri Lanka. She had taken a break from living in Los Angeles to teach in Colombo for a few years, and her children's orchestra was thriving. It was called Strings by the Sea.

Now Orlantha and I chatted in the doorway of this hotel room. We hadn't planned to come to Yala together, she was with her parents who were on holiday from the States. She watched the antics of my boys now and told me that she would love to start a family soon. "What you guys have is a dream," she said.

It was then she saw the wave. "Oh my God, the sea's coming in." That's what she said. I looked behind me. It didn't seem that remarkable. Or alarming. It was only the white curl of a big wave.

But you couldn't usually see breaking waves

from our room. You hardly noticed the ocean at all. It was just a glint of blue above that wide spread of sand that sloped sharply down to the water. Now the froth of a wave had scaled up this slope and was nearing the tall conifers that were halfway between our room and the water's edge, incongruous those trees in this landscape of brittle thorny scrub. This was peculiar. I called out to Steve in the bathroom. "Come out, Steve, I want to show you something odd." I didn't want him to miss this. I wanted him to come out quick before all this foam dissolved. "In a minute," Steve muttered, with no intention of rushing out.

Then there was more white froth. And more. Vik was sitting by the back door reading the first page of *The Hobbit.* I told him to shut that door. It was a glass door with four panels, and he closed each one, then came across the room and stood by me. He didn't say anything, he didn't ask me what was going on.

The foam turned into waves. Waves leaping over the ridge where the beach ended. This was not normal. The sea never came this far in. Waves not receding or dissolving. Closer now. Brown and gray. Brown or gray. Waves rushing past the conifers and coming closer to our room. All these waves now, charging, churning. Suddenly furious. Suddenly menacing. "Steve, you've got to come out. Now."

Steve ran out of the bathroom, tying his sarong. He looked outside. We didn't speak.

I grabbed Vik and Malli, and we all ran out the front door. I was ahead of Steve. I held the boys each by the hand. "Give me one of them. Give me one of them," Steve shouted, reaching out. But I didn't. That would have slowed us down. We had no time. We had to be fast. I knew that. But I didn't know what I was fleeing from.

I didn't stop for my parents. I didn't stop to knock on the door of my parents' room, which was next to ours, on the right as we ran out. I didn't shout to warn them. I didn't bang on their door and call them out. As I ran past, for a splintered second, I wondered if I should. But I couldn't stop. It will stall us. We must keep running. I held the boys tight by their hands. We have to get out.

We fled towards the driveway at the front of the hotel. The boys ran as fast as I did. They didn't stumble or fall. They were barefoot, but they didn't slow down because stones or thorns were hurting them. They didn't say a word. Our feet were loud, though. I could hear them, slamming the ground.

Ahead of us a jeep was moving, fast. Now it stopped. A safari jeep with open back and sides and a brown canvas hood. This jeep was waiting for us. We ran up to it. I flung Vikram into the back, and he landed facedown on the green corrugated-metal floor. Steve jumped in and picked him up. We were all inside now. Steve had Vik on his lap, I sat across from them with Malli on mine. A man was driving the jeep. I didn't know who he was.

Now I looked around me and nothing was unusual. No frothing waters here, only the hotel. It was all as it should be. The long rows of rooms with clay-tiled roofs, the terra-cotta floors of the open corridors, the dusty, orange-brown gravel driveway thick with wild cactus on both sides. All there. The waves must have receded, I thought.

I hadn't seen Orlantha run with us, but she must have done. She was in the jeep. Her parents had rushed out of their room as we came out of ours, and now her father, Anton, was with us too. Orlantha's mother, Beulah, was hoisting herself into the jeep and the driver revved the engine. The jeep jerked forward and she lost her grip, fell off. The driver didn't see this. I told him to stop, I kept yelling to him that she had fallen out. But he kept going. Beulah lay on the driveway and looked up at us as we pulled away. She half-smiled, in confusion it seemed.

Anton leaned out the back to reach Beulah and drag her up. When he couldn't, he jumped out. They were both lying on the gravel now, but I didn't call out to the driver to wait for them. He was driving very fast. He's right, I thought, we have to keep moving. Soon we will be away from the hotel.

We were leaving my parents behind. I panicked now. If I had screamed at their door as we ran out, they could have run with us. "We didn't get Aachchi and Seeya," I yelled to Steve. This made Vikram cry. Steve held on to him, clasping him to his chest. "Aachchi and Seeya will be okay, they will come later, they will come," Steve said. Vik stopped crying and snuggled into Steve.

I was thankful for Steve's words, I was reassured. Steve is right. There are no waves now. Ma and Da, they will walk out of their room. We will get out of here first, and they'll join us. I had an image of my father walking out of the hotel, there were puddles everywhere, he had his trousers rolled up. I'll ring Ma on her mobile as soon as I get to a phone, I thought.

We were nearing the end of the hotel driveway. We were about to turn left onto the dirt track that runs by the lagoon. Steve stared at the road ahead of us. He kept banging his heel on the floor of the jeep. Hurry up, get a move on.

The jeep was in water then. Suddenly, all this water inside the jeep. Water sloshing over our knees. Where did this water come from? I didn't see those waves get to us. This water must have burst out from beneath the ground. What *is* happening? The jeep moved forward slowly. I could hear its engine straining, snarling. We can drive through this water, I thought.

We were tilting from side to side. The water was rising now, filling the jeep. It came up to our chests.

Steve and I lifted the boys as high as we could. Steve held Vik, I had Mal. Their faces above the water, the tops of their heads pressing against the jeep's canvas hood, our hands tight under their armpits. The jeep rocked. It was floating, the wheels no longer gripping the ground. We kept steadying ourselves on the seats. No one spoke. No one uttered a sound.

Then I saw Steve's face. I'd never seen him like that before. A sudden look of terror, eyes wide open, mouth agape. He saw something behind me that I couldn't see. I didn't have time to turn around and look.

Because it turned over. The jeep turned over. On my side.

Pain. That was all I could feel. Where am I? Something was crushing my chest. I am trapped under the jeep, I thought, I am being flattened by it. I tried to push it away, I wanted to wriggle out. But it was too heavy, whatever was on me, the pain unrelenting in my chest.

I wasn't stuck under anything. I was moving, I could tell now. My body was curled up, I was spinning fast.

Am I underwater? It didn't feel like water, but it has to be, I thought. I was being dragged along, and my body was whipping backwards and forwards. I couldn't stop myself. When at times my eyes opened,

I couldn't see water. Smoky and gray. That was all I could make out. And my chest. It hurt like it was being pummeled by a great stone.

This is a dream. It's one of those dreams where you keep falling and falling, and then you wake up. I was sure of this now. I pinched myself. Again and again. I could feel the nip on my thigh, through my trousers. But I wasn't waking up. The water was pulling me along with a speed I did not recognize, propelling me forward with a power I could not resist. I was shoved through branches of trees and bushes, and here and there my elbows and knees smashed into something hard.

If this is not a dream, I must be dying. It can be nothing else, this terrible pain. That jeep turned over, and now something is killing me. But how can I be dying? Just now I was in our hotel room. Just now I was with the boys. My boys. My mind shook itself, it tried to focus. Vik and Malli. I *can't* die. For them, I have to stay alive.

It was too ferocious, though, the force on my chest. I only wanted for it to stop. If I am dying, please, hurry up.

But I don't want to die, our life is good, I thought. I don't want it to be over, we have much more to do, so much. Yet I had to surrender to this unknown chaos. I could sense that. I am going to die, I am nothing against whatever it is that has me in its grip. What to do, it's over, finished. I gave up. But as I went whirling in the water, I did feel disappointed that my life had to end.

This cannot be happening. Only now I was standing by the door, I was talking to Orlantha. And what was that she said? A *dream*? What you guys have is a dream. That's what she said. Her words came back to me now, I cursed her for saying that.

All at once I saw brown water. No more smoky gray, but billowing brown water, way into the distance, as far as I could see. My head was above the water now. Still I was being swept along at such a speed. There was nothing I could hold. I flung about. There are trees swirling around me. What *is* this about? I was with Vik, in our room. He wants to wear his new England cricket shirt, we are driving back to Colombo soon. I've put the shirt out on the bed. This has to be a dream, I thought. I tasted salt. Water battered my face, it went up my nose, it burned my brain. For a long while I didn't realize that the pain in my chest had stopped.

I was floating on my back. A blue spotless sky. A flock of storks was flying above me, in formation, necks stretched out. These birds were flying in the same direction that the water was taking me. Painted storks, I thought. A flight of painted storks across a Yala sky, I'd seen this thousands of times. A sight so familiar, it took me out of the mad water. Watching storks with Vik, laughing with him about their pterodactyl-like flight, for a moment or two that's where I was.

Vik and Malli, I thought again. I can't let myself die here in whatever this is. My boys.

A child was floating towards me. A boy. His head was above the water, he was screaming. Daddy, Daddy. He was clinging to something. It looked like the broken seat of a car, there was yellow foam or rubber inside. He was lying on top of it, as if he was body-boarding. From a distance, I thought this boy was Malli. I tried to reach him. The water slammed into my face and pushed me back, but I managed to get nearer to the boy. Come to Mummy, I said out loud. Then I saw his face up close. He wasn't Mal. The next instant I was knocked sideways, and the boy was gone.

I was falling through rapids. The water was plummeting. There was a man, he was being tossed about in this torrent. He was facing downwards. He had a black T-shirt on, only that. Is that Steve, I wondered, maybe it's Steve, his sarong's come off. I thought this calmly at first, and then I panicked. No, it can't be Steve. Don't let it be him.

There was a branch hanging over the water. I was floating towards it, on my back. I have to clutch that branch, I told myself, somehow I must. I knew

I'd go racing under it, so I had to lift up my arms in time to have any chance of catching it. The water thrashed my face, but I tried to keep my eyes fixed on that branch. Then I was under it, and I reached out, but the branch was nearly behind me. I threw my arms back a little and grabbed, holding on.

My feet were on the ground.

My eyes couldn't focus. But I saw then the toppled trees everywhere, I could make those out, trees on the ground with their roots sticking up. What is this, a swamp? I was in an immense bog-land. Everything was one color, brown, reaching far. This didn't look like Yala, where the ground is dry and cracked and covered in green shrub. What is this knocked-down world? The end of time?

I was bent double, I couldn't straighten. I held my knees, I was panting hard, choking. There was sand in my mouth. I wretched and coughed up blood. I kept spitting and spitting. So much salt. My body felt very heavy. My trousers, they are weighing me down, I thought. I took them off. What happened to those waves? There are pools of still water around me, but no waves. Are these lakes or lagoons?

I couldn't keep steady. My feet sank in sludge. I stared into this unknown landscape, still wondering if I was dreaming, but fearing, almost knowing, I was not.

It was only then that I wondered what happened

to everyone. Could they be dead? They must be. They must be dead. What am I going to do without them, I thought. Still panting, still spitting. I couldn't keep balance, I was sliding in mud.

I heard voices. Distant at first, then close. It was a group of men, shouting to each other in Sinhala. They couldn't see me, or me them. One of them said, "*Muhuda goda gahala. Mahasona avilla.*" The ocean has flooded. Mahasona is here. Mahasona. I knew the word, but what was he saying? I had last heard that word when I was a child and our nanny told us stories about ghouls and demons. Mahasona, he is the demon of graveyards. Even in my complete bewilderment, I understood. Something dreadful had happened, there was death everywhere, that's what the man was shouting about.

That voice called out again. "Is anyone here, you can come out now, the water's gone, we are here to help." I didn't budge or make a sound. I felt too exhausted to speak. Then a child's voice, "Help me. Save me. I was washed away." I heard the men come closer to find the child. I stayed silent. Bent over, holding my knees.

The men spotted me and ran over. They spoke to me, but I didn't reply. They said I should go with them, we must hurry, there could be another wave. I kept shaking my head and refusing. I was too tired. And without my boys, how could I leave? What if they'd survived? They might be near here somewhere, I couldn't leave them behind. But I couldn't say this out loud. I couldn't ask these men to search for them. I couldn't tell them that we had been thrown out of the jeep into that water. Telling them would make it too real.

The men were impatient. They talked among themselves. They couldn't leave me here. "But we can't take her like this," one of them said. "She has no trousers on." What? I thought. He took off his shirt and tied it around my waist. They pulled me along, I still felt heavy, my legs dragged through mud. It was deep, knee-high slime. A few times I fell over, and they hauled me up.

We saw a man lying under a bush. He was wearing only a loincloth. One of the men with me went up to him. He's dead, he came back and said. He mentioned a name, and I recognized it. He was a fisherman who lived in a small hut on the beach by the hotel. Steve and I would talk to him, he would try to sell conch shells to the boys, they'd press those shells against their ears to listen to the hum of the ocean. I looked away from this man, now motionless in the sand. I didn't want to see anyone dead.

They took me to a van, and we drove a short distance. When the van stopped, I knew where I was. We were at the ticket office at the entrance to the national park. I knew this building well. I'd been here hundreds of times, since I was a child, to buy tickets and to pick up a ranger to guide us in the park. Vik and Malli sometimes went into the small museum in this building, at the entrance to it was an enormous pair of elephant tusks.

The building looked no different now. All intact. No trace of water, no puddles or uprooted trees around it. This dry breeze on my face, it's a normal breeze.

The men carried me out of the van and took me inside. I knew several people who worked here, I could see them now, milling around, staring at me, looking concerned. I turned away from them. I didn't want them to see me like this, shaking, sopping wet.

I sat on a green concrete bench in the museum, which had half-walls with peeling green paint and thick wooden pillars that held up the roof. I hugged my knees into my chest and stared at the *palu* trees outside. Was it real, what just happened, that water? My crumpled mind couldn't tell. And I wanted to stay in the unreal, in the not knowing. So I didn't speak to anyone, ask them anything. A phone began to ring. No one picked it up, so it rang and rang. It was loud, and I wanted it to stop. I wanted to stay in my stupor, staring into trees.

But what if they survived, I couldn't help thinking. Steve might come here with the boys. Maybe someone found all of them, just as they found me. If they are brought here, the boys will be clinging to Steve. Daddy, Daddy. Their shirts would have been torn off, they will be cold. Vik would always be shaking and shivering when he went swimming, the water in the pool was a little bit chilly.

A white truck pulled up. A young girl was carried out. There were bruises on her face, and twigs and leaves stuck to her hair and clothes. I'd seen this girl before. She was in the room next to us in the hotel with her parents. Vik and Malli will look wet and scared like this girl if they are brought here now. Will they have leaves tangled in their hair? They both had haircuts before we left London. Haircuts. I couldn't hold the thought of haircuts.

There was a boy sitting on the same bench as me. He looked about twelve, a little older maybe. This was the boy who called for help just before those men found me. They brought him here with me in that van. This boy wouldn't stop talking now, shouting. Where are his parents, he wants them, he was having breakfast with them at the hotel, they saw the waves, they ran, he was swept away. He said this over and over, but I ignored him. I didn't acknowledge his presence or respond to anything he said.

The boy began to cry now. Are his parents dead? he asked. He was wearing only a pair of shorts, and his body was shaking, and his teeth chattered, and he kept walking around the glass cabinets, which displayed skeletons of marsh crocodiles and pythons. There was also the nest of a weaverbird, which always intrigued Vik. "It's like a real house, Malli. Can you see the different rooms?"

The boy kept walking back and forth and crying. I wanted him to stop. Someone brought a large towel and wrapped it around his shoulders. Still the boy sobbed. But I didn't speak to him. I didn't try to comfort him. Stop blubbing, I thought, shut up. You only survived because you are fat. That's why you didn't die. You stayed alive in that water because you are so fucking fat. Vik and Malli didn't have a chance. Just shut up.

I was taken to the hospital in a jeep. The man driving was very agitated. He told me he didn't know where his family was. He was going to the hospital to look for them. They had been staying at the hotel, same as us. But he went on safari early in the morning. He went alone. He wasn't at the hotel when the wave struck. He told me this again and again. He spoke too loudly. I sat in the front seat next to him. I didn't say a word. I shivered and I shook. I stared out of the jeep. The road we were driving on was bordered by thick forest. There was no one on that road but us.

There was another man sitting at the back of the jeep. I recognized him, he was a waiter in our hotel. The waiter had a mobile phone in his hand, he kept waving it about. He stuck his hand out of the jeep and held the phone up high. He jumped across the seats from side to side. He was trying to get a signal, he said. His movements, I couldn't stand it, I could feel each thud. Why can't you just sit still, I kept thinking. I wanted to fling his phone out of that jeep.

They could already be at the hospital. Steve and the boys. Even Ma and Da. They might have been found and taken there. I kept thinking this, then stifling the thought. I had to stop getting my hopes up. I won't find them, I must prepare for this. But if they *were* there, they'd be worried about me. I wished the jeep would speed up.

When we got to the hospital, it was Anton, Orlantha's father, who came rushing out. He had no shirt, his trousers were ripped, his toes were bloody. He peered into the jeep, looking confused. Why is Orlantha not with you? Where are Steve and the boys? he asked. He thought this was the same jeep we'd driven off in, leaving him lying on the ground. I told him it wasn't, that I didn't know where anyone was. I didn't tell him I'd hoped they'd be at the hospital. Now that I was sure they were not.

I dragged myself into the waiting area. My legs felt battered, they were unsteady. I noticed deep scratches on my ankles, they were bleeding, there were cuts on the soles of my feet. What happened? My mind could not sort anything out.

All around me people were talking. I didn't want to speak to anyone, so I didn't look their way. The waiting room was small, but their voices seemed distant, they kept getting softer and trailing off. Someone tapped me on the shoulder. It was a tidal wave, there was a tidal wave, he said. I nodded. I tried to seem casual, as if I'd known all along. But a tidal wave is real. My heart tumbled. I sat down on a wooden bench in a corner, by a wall, facing the entrance to the hospital.

They might still come. We don't get tidal waves

in Sri Lanka. These people don't know what they're talking about. An image of Steve walking in with Vik and Mal kept sparking in my head. All three of them bare-chested, Steve carrying the boys, one on each arm. But they couldn't have survived, they just couldn't, I kept warning myself. Yet I silently and hopelessly murmured, there might, *might* just be the smallest chance.

Now and then a van or a truck came through the hospital gates. Everything very fast. Doors slammed, there was shouting, people staggered out from the trucks, others were carried, nurses and doctors ran outside clattering stretchers and wheelchairs down a ramp. A woman was brought in and left in front of my bench. She had long hair that was matted, it spread across her face. She was mumbling, but she wasn't making sense. She was covered with a sheet because she was naked, but her feet stuck out, and they were crusted with mud. I couldn't stop staring at her. I wondered if it was seaweed, all that slime twisted in her hair.

Anton was also in the waiting room. Each time a truck pulled up, he looked expectant. He rushed out. He went to see if it was bringing his family, or mine. I didn't budge. I didn't want to be so quickly disappointed, like Anton was. Always he came back inside within moments, shaking his head. Now and again a child was brought in. These were other children, not Vik and Mal. I watched as each empty truck drove away. They can't be alive, they were not even in that one.

The gashes on my ankles hurt. A nurse asked me to come inside and have them cleaned and dressed. I ignored her. Sod off, leave me alone, I thought. Why do these scratches matter? When something this horrendous has happened, I don't even know what. Anton kept walking around talking to the doctors and nurses. They bandaged the cuts on his toes. He kept praising the hospital staff to me, even with these meager facilities they were coping remarkably well in this chaos. He knew, he was a doctor, he knew they were doing a great job. Like I care, I thought.

Those benches became crowded. It was stuffy and hot. But I had to sit tight, I couldn't go outside. If I moved, I would lose my space. And I wanted my corner. I could lean against that wall.

I was still wet. The nurse I'd just ignored asked me to change my top. She brought me a T-shirt. I wanted to change, but I couldn't figure out where to do it. I'm not going into one of those toilets, they'll stink. I felt nauseated at the thought. So I peeled off my soggy blue shirt right where I was sitting and dropped it on the floor between the bench and the wall. I put on the dry T-shirt. It was purple, and on the front it had a smiling yellow teddy bear.

Some people passing through that waiting room recognized me. Jeep drivers who saw us regularly in

the park, a few waiters from the hotel. They came
up to me looking concerned, they asked where my
family was, where were my children, hadn't I seen
any one of them yet. I shrugged, shook my head. I
wanted them to leave me alone. Each time someone
approached me, I was terrified I'd be told that Steve
or the boys or my parents were dead.

The man who was the masseur at our hotel
walked past my bench. I'd had a massage with him
the previous day, a nice Christmas treat. I had it out-
doors on the veranda in the heat of the afternoon, a
dry breeze blew in from the sea. Vik played with his
cricket ball on the side, bowling to a chair standing
in for Steve who was having a nap. Malli sipped a
Sprite wearing a Santa hat with flashing lights. That
tacky hat Steve got from Tally-Ho Discount in North
Finchley, knowing that Malli would be impressed.
I thought of all this, then quickly shut out these
thoughts. I couldn't think about yesterday now.
Not in this madness, not if they were dead. Fucking
Tally-Ho Discount, I always hated that shop.

And it irked me when I saw that masseur. He
didn't look injured, he didn't even look wet. How did
he survive? I thought. Vik and Mal probably didn't,
so why did he? Whenever I recognized someone from
the hotel, I thought this. Why are they alive, surely
that wave should have got them as well. Why aren't
they dead?

When Mette turned up at the hospital, I was

thankful to see him. I felt a little safer now. Mette is a jeep driver, and he always drove us on safari in the park. We'd known him a long time. We had said goodbye to him the previous night when he took us back to the hotel. It had been an uneventful safari, only a blur of a bear at dusk. We told him we'd see him again in August, we were leaving the next day. August is not that long to wait, I told Vik, who was always impatient to return. Now Mette was at the hospital because someone had told him that I was here, alone. He sat with me on the bench, he didn't bother me with any questions. I asked him what time it was. It was around noon.

The vans and trucks stopped coming in through those gates after a while. The waiting room fell silent, it emptied out. I couldn't take this quiet, it was better with the rushing and shouting and talking. At least something was happening then. I was jittery now, nothing going on, so I asked Mette if he could take me back to Yala. He agreed. I should go back in case they are waiting for me there, I told myself. They won't be, they won't be, I know. But still I should go check.

I walked barefoot to Mette's jeep. The gravel outside was burning hot and the cuts on the soles of my feet stung. We drove through Tissa town. Every shop was shut, but the streets were teeming. I heard voices on loudspeakers, urgent. People were piled into the trailers of tractors that were speeding this way and that. Mette's jeep crawled the fifteen or so miles to Yala. When we turned into the road leading to the park entrance, I couldn't recognize it. This road usually went through scrub jungle. Now on either side was an endless marsh.

There was no one waiting at the ticket office, I could tell as we approached it. One of the park rangers came up to our jeep. Everyone who had been found alive was taken to the hospital, he said. But there were bodies near the hotel, if we wanted to go identify. Mette looked at me, indicating he would do it. But there was no way I would let him. What would I do if I learned they were dead? We turned around to go back to the hospital. It was getting late now, I could feel my hope dissolve.

We stopped at the police station in Tissa on the way, to check if they had a phone that worked. All the phone lines had been down since morning. It was Mette's idea for me to call someone in Colombo, but I didn't want to, I couldn't face telling anyone what had happened. I stayed in the jeep in the front yard of the police station while Mette went inside.

It was cooler now. From the shadows falling long across the paddy fields that surrounded the police station, I knew it was around five o'clock. Five o'clock. This is the time Vik plays cricket with Steve, I thought. I could hear Vik bouncing a ball, throwing it extra hard onto the ground as he would do, to give himself a difficult catch. He always squinted and smiled while waiting for the ball to drop into his hands. I thought of this but I couldn't get his face into focus, it was blurred. When I was sitting in the hospital hoping they'd come in, I could see them clearly, but I couldn't now. Mette returned and told me that even the police didn't have a phone that worked. That's a relief, I thought.

There was a child sitting in an ambulance outside the hospital when we returned. A doctor was shouting, does anyone know this child, does this child belong to anyone here? The doctor wanted to send the child to another hospital some distance away. I tottered up to the ambulance. The back doors were open, I looked in. Is this a boy or a girl? I couldn't say. Is this child older or younger than Malli? I couldn't say. Is this Malli? I just couldn't say for sure. It might be. Probably not. People gathered around the ambulance. They looked at me silently. They looked at me trying to decide if this was my son. I touched the child's leg. Does this feel like Mal? I couldn't tell. It might be Mal, and they are going to send him away. Then I remembered, Malli had a dark brown birthmark halfway down the outside of his left thigh. A birthspot, he called it. "Mum, do you have a birthspot also?" he would ask.

I could hear his voice now. "It's on yer bum! Ugh, Dad, look, Mummy's birthspot is on her bum!" "It's not *on* my bum, Mal, it's *near* my bum. It's on my back." I looked at the child's left thigh, and there was no round brown mark. I looked at the right thigh as well, just in case. I went back inside the waiting room and took my place in the corner of that bench, by the wall.

The room filled up again. There were people crying and holding on to each other, some were slumped against pillars, some crouched on the floor with their heads in their hands. The person next to me was pressing on me, there were many more people now squeezed tight on the bench. All around me it reeked of sweat and more sweat. I tried to free myself from the smell by turning my face to the wall. Outside it was dark. When did this happen? I trembled. The light had fled.

The same nurse from the morning saw me and came over. She stroked my head, she knew my children were missing, she said. I stiffened, I didn't want to see her look sad for me. Now she was going to make me cry, and I didn't want that. I hadn't shed a tear all day, and I wasn't going to. Not with all these people here, not now.

A truck pulled in. Its headlights swung across the front yard of the hospital. They've found more survivors even though it's late, they are bringing them in. For a moment that's what I thought. But then it erupted. The scream. In an instant everyone in that room surged to the entrance. They howled in unison, shoving each other, pushing forward, desperate arms stretched out. Some policeman arrived and pushed them back. But the wailing went on. No words, just an unending, rising, screaming scream. Then I knew. This truck was different. It was bodies this truck had brought.

I'd never heard shrieking like this before. So wild, wretched, it frightened me, rattled the wall I was holding on to. This noise was crackling into the numbness in my head. It was blasting the smallest stir of hope in my heart. It was telling me that what had happened was unthinkable, but I didn't want this confirmed. Not by wailing strangers, I did not.

I pushed my way through the crowd, I had to escape this din, I had to go outside. As I neared the front entrance, a policeman trying to calm the crowd yelled out, "These bodies are not your people, they are only tourists from the hotel." I didn't flinch when I heard him. I focused on getting out. I moved through the throng of people as if his words did not matter. I didn't drop to the ground. I didn't even whimper, though it was now my turn to scream.

I stumbled into Mette's jeep, parked under a lamppost by the front gates. It was quiet in there. I sat in the driver's seat and put my head down on the steering wheel. The bodies are from the hotel, the policeman said.

Anton found me in the jeep. I still had my head on the steering wheel when I heard his voice. I didn't grasp what he was saying at first. Then I heard the word mortuary, and I balked. Does he want me to go to the mortuary? He can't be serious, is he out of his mind? I knew I couldn't step in there, no way. I couldn't even think the thought, *What if Vik and Mal are there?* Even though it hovered unformed in my head.

When I finally understood what Anton was asking, I was thrown. He wanted me to push him to the mortuary in a wheelchair. A wheelchair? Then he explained. The wounds on his feet were too painful, he couldn't walk that far. So could I wheel him there? My mind was mangled. I have to push him through rows of dead people in a wheelchair? I told him I couldn't do it. He pleaded, and I kept refusing, for a while at least. But I was tired, I was beaten. Any resolve I had quickly waned, and I gave in.

The wheelchair was heavy. I had to maneuver it through the crowd. I was furious at having to do this and rammed it into whoever was in my path. Anton gave me directions, and I pushed him along an open corridor, all the time thinking, this cannot be really happening, it surely cannot. Is this me, with an old blanket around my waist, pushing a wheelchair to a mortuary where my entire family might be? Then Anton pointed to a room. I'm not going in, I'm not going near the place, I thought. I let go of the wheelchair and saw it roll down the sloped corridor towards the room. I found my way to the jeep and sat in the dark.

Anton came back, I don't know how much later. He stood by the window of the jeep. He found Orlantha, he told me. He found her, only her. She is not with us anymore, she is gone, he said.

His face was empty. I held his hand. This is getting real now, I thought. Slowly, very slowly, the realness of what was unfolding was seeping into my brain. I knew then I had to go back to Colombo. There will be more trucks coming in through the night, more bodies. I had to get out.

Mette agreed to take me to Colombo. His jeep was too decrepit for the journey, he had to find us a car. He turned on his phone, and for the first time that day there was a signal. He gave me the phone. I rang my mother's mobile. That's the first thing I did, still thinking there was a possibility it might ring, that they might even answer. But they did not. There was only that recording in Sinhala, the number you have called is not responding. Mette then suggested I call my aunt's house. I did so reluctantly, I punched the numbers on the keypad slowly. How do I explain, what do I say? My cousin Krishan answered. The connection was bad, there was a lot of interference. I mumbled something like, it's only me who survived, I'm coming back. The phone went dead, again the signal was gone.

Mette took me to his home, which was very near the hospital, on a quiet street. There was a well in his front garden, by the side of a large tree. I could hear splashing in the dark, someone was taking a bath. Mette's wife and daughter were home. He told them to look after me, he was taking me to Colombo, he was going out to find us a car.

I sat on a brown leather armchair in their living room. The two women sat on the sofa next to me. They offered me food and drink. I said I didn't want anything. They insisted and brought me a cup of very sweet tea. I sipped it, it tasted nice. I held the cup with both hands, that warmth felt good.

They asked me about what happened. I'd hoped they wouldn't, but they did. When did we see the wave, where were we then, what did it look like, did it roar, where did I run to, where did I last see my kids. I didn't reply. There was a big clock on the table across from me. I sat cross-legged on the armchair and ogled that clock. I could see they were shaken and upset for me, these women, but I didn't want to speak. I wanted to fade into that chair.

The women began to lament my plight. Never in their lives had they heard such a story, everyone dying and just one person left. She's lost her children, she's lost her world, how can she live? And her children, they were so beautiful. If they were me, the women wailed, they wouldn't be sitting quietly, they'd be out of their minds, most likely they would have died of grief. I said nothing. My eyes clung to that clock.

The front door of the house was open, neighbors and relatives wandered in. They were told about me. Everyone looked at me aghast. She's lost her children? And her husband and her parents? Some of the visitors left quickly and returned with more people saying, look at this poor lady, isn't it unbelievable, her whole family is gone. I was slumped in that brown armchair. Is this me they are talking about?

Someone pointed to the cuts on my face and arms and legs. Everyone looked anxious and worried. I might get an infection, why didn't I have my wounds cleaned up at the hospital, they asked. I shrugged. Then there was concern because I didn't want food. I might faint if I don't eat, after what I've been through. Where was Mette? I wished he'd hurry up. I wondered if the hands on that clock were stuck.

At one time everyone in that house began to panic. What if that wave comes back tonight, it could kill them all. It was an elderly man who set this ranting off when he wheeled his bike into the house. They were too afraid to sleep tonight. This is it, they will all be engulfed, probably soon, you never know when. Don't be silly, I thought to myself, you live about twenty miles away from the sea. But I didn't have the energy to allay their fears, I couldn't open my mouth to talk.

Some three long hours later Mette returned with a van. The owner of the van would drive us to Colombo. It was close to midnight. Finally I could stop watching that clock. I felt huge relief when I first climbed into that van. But as we began driving in the darkness, I was scared. I didn't want to get to Colombo. I wanted to escape the madness of the hospital, I wanted to get away from everyone at Mette's house, but couldn't I somehow *stay* suspended in my confusion? I want to sit in the back of this moving van forever. In a few hours it will be light. It will be tomorrow. I don't want it to be tomorrow. I was terrified that tomorrow the truth would start.

*A*t first I ignored the crunching in my ears as I was waking up. Then I knew what it was. It was Vikram eating a pack of crisps. The slow crunch, crunch and the rustle of foil as he took a single crisp out of the pack, savored it with his eyes, lowered it into his mouth, and munched. And he repeated this until the last little smashed-up piece of crisp was gone. That was how he ate crisps. With unhurried, exaggerated actions to demonstrate just how much he relished them. His behavior was even more emphatic if I was around, to call attention to my cruelty, in not allowing him a daily ration of his favorite snack. *But, Mum,* other kids have crisps in their packed lunch every day. Yes, *every* single day, and *I* have to eat a stupid muesli bar. *Yuk.* The noises in my ears went on and on, and I lay there immobilized. Vikram's revenge, I thought, getting back at me for all the times I deprived him of junk food. Then I could see him, sitting on a pillow on my bed, wearing his school clothes, gray trousers and bright red sweater. Leaning back on the headboard, his knees tucked up, holding a packet of Tesco Ready Salted Crisps in his left hand. He has his gray school socks on, the long ones with stripes on them, threadbare at the big toes. It was the after-school look. Mud stains on the trousers, a trace of dried-up snot below one nostril. Don't drop crumbs on my pillow, I'd say. Don't sit on my bed with your mucky school trousers on. Go wash your hands now, Vik.

Wave

I climbed out of the van that stopped by the gates of my aunt's house. It was three a.m., the middle of the first night after the wave. I dusted crumbs off my clothes. Somewhere along the way the driver of the van had stopped to buy some biscuits. I told him I didn't want Lemon Puffs, so he bought Ginger Nuts.

There was a crowd gathered at the house. They rushed out as I arrived. I saw my uncle Bala at the front. He lifted his hands to his head when he saw me, he opened his mouth as though he was about to howl. I quickly turned away, staggering past everyone and going upstairs. I needed to shower, there were stones in my hair.

I sat on the bed in my cousin Natasha's room. I held on to the covers I'd pulled up to my chin. My relatives and friends asked me questions. I told them the jeep turned over in the water. I described the crushing in my chest. Didn't I see Ma or Da or Steve or Vik or Malli? they kept asking. In the water? Any *one* of them? They couldn't have survived, I heard myself insist. I was prodding myself to say this, to think this. I must prepare for when I know it's true, I thought.

I asked for a hot drink. Someone brought tea.

Someone suggested I take a sleeping pill. I refused the pill. How can I sleep? If I sleep now I will forget. I will forget what happened. I will wake believing everything is fine. I will reach for Steve, I will wait for my boys. Then I will remember. And that will be too awful. That I must not risk.

My aunt asked me for Steve's parents' telephone number. This unnerved me. I got the numbers right but muddled the order. I was troubled by this talk of calling Steve's family. It meant something was wrong and I didn't want to admit to that. Earlier when I looked in the bathroom mirror and saw shocking purple bruises streaking my face, I promptly looked away. This was needless proof, this was far too real. I wanted to stay dangling in a dream. Even though I knew I was not.

It's possible Steve is alive. He has the boys. He will phone us. His voice will be tired. I could hear it, *Hello, Sonal,* barely audible. I didn't reveal these thoughts to anyone.

The gluey dark snot coming out of my nose reeked of dog shit. My forehead was being drilled. The next morning my aunt called a doctor. A bit pointless, I thought, I will kill myself soon. The doctor dropped his bag as he walked into the room, and it fell open, and his instruments rattled onto the floor. He stuck them into my nose and my ears and my throat. A raging infection, in my sinuses, that filthy water. He gave me five types of antibiotics.

I should inhale steam. It will clear the gunk. It will lessen the pain.

The stunned voices of friends and family floated about. An earthquake under the sea near Indonesia. The tectonic plates shifted. It's the biggest natural disaster ever. A tsunami. Until now our killer had for me been nameless. This was the first time I'd ever heard the word. They talked numbers. A hundred thousand dead, two hundred thousand, a quarter of a million. I was unmoved. I cowered on that bed. It could be a million more for all *I* care, I thought.

They meant nothing, those words, tsunami, tidal wave. Something came for us. I didn't know what it was then, and I still didn't. How can something so unknown do this? How can my family be dead? We were in our hotel room?

I can't live without them. I can't. Can't.

Why didn't I die? Why did I cling to that branch?

Pieces of me hovered in a murky netherworld, timeless day after timeless day.

I don't remember when they told me. Three, four, five days later. I had limped downstairs. There were thorns deep in my feet, and they were now rising to the surface, almost piercing the skin when my feet touched the floor.

"They found Ma and Da today," my brother Rajiv said softly. I sat down. The chair was broken and I tipped backwards and nearly fell off. Someone rushed to give me another chair. I looked at Rajiv. "They found Ma and Da," he said again. I knew what he meant. He meant they'd found their bodies.

"And I think also Vik," he said. "Can you remember what he was wearing? Was it a green T-shirt and black and white shorts, checked ones?" I nodded. He is telling me that Vik is dead. I stared at Rajiv and my aunt and my uncle and Natasha, who were in the room. He is telling me that Vik is dead. I stared, wordless. That green T-shirt, it had a tiger on it, we got it in India, it was the day we saw a wild tiger for the first time. He is telling me that Vik is dead? I didn't scream or wail. I didn't faint. And I didn't think of asking for them to keep that green T-shirt.

I'll wait until all the bodies are found, I told myself. Then I will kill myself.

My brother organized a massive search for Malli. Malli just might be alive. He scoured the country with friends and family. They went to every hospital, every camp for survivors, they appealed in the newspapers and on TV, they offered rewards. Malli's photo looked out from walls and shop windows and the back of trishaws. I pretended to ignore Rajiv's efforts. I told myself they were in vain. I must not hope. Not again, not now.

How can I accept that Steve and Mal just vanished? That there will never be any proof? I kept asking myself this. How can I tolerate something so absurd? But then, all that was reasonable in this world had been blasted by that wave.

They are my world. How do I make them dead? My mind toppled.

In a stupor I began to teach myself the impossible. I had to learn it even by rote. We will not fly back to London. The boys will not be at school on Tuesday. Steve will not call me from work to ask if I took them in on time. Vik will not play tag outside his classroom again. Malli will not skip in a circle with some little girls. The Gruffalo. Malli will not cuddle me in bed and read about the Gruffalo, with that poisonous wart at the end of its nose. Vik will not be excited by whoever scored for Liverpool. They will not peep into the oven to check if my apple crumble has cooked. My chant went on.

But I could not absorb any of it.

I'd put pizzas in the freezer for the boys because our flight got into Heathrow late. The milkman will deliver our usual the next morning, I'd left a note. We are going to a party at Anita's on New Year's Eve. It was Christmas. Vik and Malli were singing their favorite version of "Jingle Bells," squealing out the line "Uncle Billy lost his willy on the motorway." Not long ago they were giddy with Halloween. Their left-over bounty of sweeties is still in an orange bucket in the kitchen. I can feel their gloved fingers twining mine. It's fireworks night, I can smell damp November on their cheeks.

All that they were missing, I desperately shut out. I was terrified of everything because everything was from that life. Anything that excited them, I wanted destroyed. I panicked if I saw a flower. Malli would have stuck it in my hair. I couldn't tolerate a blade of grass. That's where Vik would have stamped. At dusk I shuddered when I glimpsed the thousands of bats and crows that crisscrossed the Colombo sky. I wanted them extinct, they belonged in my old life, that display always thrilled my boys.

Now I had to make myself safe. I had to shrink my sight. I disappeared into darkness. I shut myself in the room. Even with the curtains closed, I pulled the covers over my head.

The traffic outside my aunt's house was endless. The noise stripped my nerves. But it felt fitting to be in that grueling din. I could better make them dead when I was constantly jolted like this. These were the warped sounds of life without them. From our bedroom in London we mostly heard finches and robins and the thump of a football.

London, the thought of it, I felt horror. Our home. Their school. Their friends. Taking the Pic-

cadilly Line to the Natural History Museum. The
jingle of the ice-cream van. What do I do with all
this? I wanted to shred my knowledge of our life.

I was frightened of Sundays. It was just after
nine on a Sunday morning that the wave came for
us. Now I tried not to look at a clock on a Sunday
morning. I didn't want to know that it was exactly
at this time two, three, four, ten, fifteen weeks before
that life ended, for them, for us. In Colombo we
went swimming on Sunday mornings. Now I steeled
myself against the sensation of Malli's silky earlobes
on my cheek as I held him in the deep. Now I didn't
want to acknowledge that it was a Sunday morning
and Vik would never again have a tantrum because
Steve was reading the papers and not taking him to
the park. That it was a Sunday morning and Steve
would never again smear newsprint on the toilet
seat.

This could not have happened to me. This is
not me. I teetered endlessly. Look at me, powerless,
a plastic bag in a gale.

This is not me. I'd lumber into the shower, and
unable to work out how to get the water going,
I'd stare at the taps and get dressed again, squirm
back into bed. I felt I was falling and falling as I lay
motionless on that bed, plummeting so fast I had
to grip the sides.

How is this me? I was safe always. Now I don't
have them, I only have terror, I am alone. My stom-

ach cramped. I pressed a hot water bottle to my
chest to calm the hammer blows to my heart, but
they wouldn't stop.

I stabbed myself with a butter knife. I lashed at
my arms and my thighs. I smashed my head on the
sharp corner of the wooden headboard of the bed. I
stubbed out cigarettes on my hands. I didn't smoke,
I only burned them into my skin. Again and again.
My boys.

I don't have them to hold. What do I do with my
arms?

Soon, very soon, I have to kill myself.

I was never left alone. An army of family and
friends guarded me night and day.

Natasha kept hold of me, not leaving my side
for half that year. Ramani infuriated me by tapping
on the bathroom door if she thought I was taking a
suspiciously long time, but my body was so clenched
that I had to sit on the toilet with all the taps running for ages just to pee. I chased Keshini out of
the bedroom at night, accusing her of snoring too
loud, yet she took six months off from her job in the
States to watch over me. Amrita warmed me and distracted me, her job abandoned, children left in other
people's care. Gunna and Darini coaxed me to take a
few steps outside that room. Ruri snuggled into bed
with me to cry.

Sometimes I would drag myself into the
kitchen—maybe I can slit my wrists—but someone

would steal up behind me. Besides, they had hidden all the knives. My aunt gave me a sleeping pill at night, carefully rationed, just one. I tried to hoard them, together with some bottles of painkillers I'd found. Then Natasha discovered my stash and yelled at me like I was a bicycle thief. I thought every day about throwing myself under one of the buses that hurtled by outside. But Natasha assured me that if I didn't succeed and instead became paralyzed, she would leave me all day in my wheelchair in the middle of the garden, alone.

I insisted I never wanted to see our friends in London or Steve's family again. That life was over. But they turned up.

When our friend Lester walked into my blackened room and told me he was so glad I was alive, I shouted at him. Didn't he get it, stupid man, I wanted to die. Lester had been in Colombo with us only a few months before, in the summer. We'd gone to cricket matches where he impressed Vik by drinking too much beer. We went to the rain forest where Malli woke him too early each morning to go for a walk. And now Lester is here because they are all dead?

I was bewildered when Anita appeared sobbing in my room. We'd said goodbye to each other after the school Christmas concert weeks before, shouting at our children not to trip on their costumes as they raced down the road. And now? Anita kept telling me that I had to live, without me she couldn't raise her girls. Fuck off, I thought.

Steve's family came to Colombo, again and again. When his brother-in-law Chris began telling me about the memorial service they were planning in London, I asked him to stop. Memorial service? That was outlandish. Still he persisted, asking me to choose some music for the service, cajoling me gently by mentioning that my mother-in-law had remarked, "Well, when Stephen was a boy he liked some band called Slade." I braced myself and told Chris to play some Coltrane. Just saying that word made my heart convulse. I saw Steve in our kitchen, grilling fish, listening to *A Love Supreme.*

Steve's sister Beverley sat on my bed wiping her tears. On the morning of the twenty-sixth of December, she had woken up in London, weeping. At the time she hadn't been able to imagine a reason for this, it was the morning after Christmas, they'd had a typically happy and raucous family gathering the previous day. But before someone phoned her with news of a tidal wave in Sri Lanka, she had been crying. As she told me this, I could only think, her chin, her chin, her chin is Steve's.

I didn't want to step out of that room. The only time I willingly raised myself from that bed was to go to the bathroom to brush my teeth. I brushed my teeth diligently and often. I shuffled to the bathroom every few hours and carefully squeezed toothpaste onto my brush. I brushed hard. My arm hurt, but I kept going, "giving it some welly," as Steve would say. I tried not to think of Steve's words as I looked in the mirror and focused on my frothy mouth. I liked the sound of my frantic brushing, but I hated the toothpaste, it tasted of cloves and made me gag.

I resolved not to leave the house, ever. How can I go outside? Outside was where I went with my boys. How can I walk without holding on to them, one on each side?

There were all those first times. The first time I came downstairs in my aunt's house, frightened, knowing I wouldn't see a heap of shoes by the front door, as there was at home. The first time I walked on a Colombo street and couldn't bear to glimpse a child, a ball. The first time I visited a friend and was nearly physically sick. Steve and I had been here with the boys just weeks before, my children's finger-prints were on her wall. The first time I saw money, I was with my friend David, who wanted to buy a comb, having come from England without one. I trembled as I peered at that hundred-rupee note in his hand. The last time I saw one of those, I had a world.

There was the first time I saw a paradise fly-catcher. I thought then I should never have allowed my friends to open the curtains in my room. I had been much safer in blackness. Now sunlight splintered my eyes, and that familiar bird trailed its fiery feathers along the branches of the tamarind tree outside. No sooner I saw it, I turned away. Now look what's happened, I thought. I've seen a bird. I've seen a flycatcher, when all the birds in the world should be dead.

The first time I saw a photo of my boys, I was unprepared. I was searching the Internet for ways of killing myself, as I often did then, when one click led to another, until the London *Evening Standard* screamed, "I watched as my whole family was swept away," alongside a large photo of Vik and Mal. That photo, it was taken at school, Malli wore a red shirt, and he was proud. An image I knew so well overwhelmed me now. My mind had not fixed on their faces since the wave, it couldn't endure them. I fell on the bed and pressed a pillow over my face.

And that headline, "I watched"? I hadn't spoken to any journalist, I had barely left that room. How dare they? I seethed. If Steve was here, if Steve was here, I'd tell him to go find those *Evening Standard* journalists on a dark night and beat them to a pulp.

Steve and Malli were identified four months after the wave. All that while I'd told myself that they'd disappeared into the depths of the ocean. Vanished. Magically became extinct. This kept their deaths as unreal and as dreamlike as the wave. Then at the end of April, I was told that they had both been identified by DNA testing. It was just days before Steve's birthday. He would have been forty-one.

I didn't know then that their bodies had been exhumed from a mass grave sometime in February. I didn't know that the DNA testing was being done in a laboratory somewhere in Austria. When I was told they were found, I smashed things into pieces. I didn't want them to be found now. Not as dead bodies. I didn't want them in coffins.

I went to that mass grave with David later that year. It was a scruffy plot of land next to a Buddhist temple in Kirinda, a few miles from Yala. Some children from the village rushed over and told me more than I wanted to hear. "The bodies were brought at night, in tractors and bulldozers," they said. "Some were clothed, some were not. No clothes at all. The people in the village were scared, but the priest in the temple allowed the bodies to be buried. Then the police came one day, some of them were white policemen, and dug it up. They told us not to watch, but we did."

I didn't tell them I did not want to hear this. I didn't walk away. I just listened. It was Steve and Mal they were talking about. Steve and Mal. "My mother went mad when she saw the dead bodies," said one of the boys. "We had a *thovila* for her and everything, a *kattadiya*"—a sorcerer—"even came. We had to pay him twenty-five thousand rupees. But she is still not cured. Still mad."

Wave

We had left London on the night of the eighth of December. Steve and I worked from home that day. At lunchtime we drove to Muswell Hill, did some shopping. We went to the music store, Vik needed a book for the piano exam he was taking in April. We bought a Keith Jarrett CD, *The Melody at Night, With You*. We shared some chocolate cake at Oliver's Deli. We popped into M&S because we'd been overcharged for some wine at the weekend, we'd bought three bottles but were charged for five. The cashier asked if we wanted cash back or a credit voucher. Steve said a voucher's fine, we'll always come back here. He put that voucher in his wallet.

The school Christmas concert had been the previous night. It was *A Christmas Carol*. Vikram stood at the back and sang listlessly as usual. Malli sat on Steve's knee in the audience. When they sang "White Christmas," he sang along. His face was a picture, enchanted by the fake snow falling on the stage. Malli loved all things snowy. I must take him to see *The Snowman* at the Peacock Theatre when we get back from Colombo, I decided then. I'd seen him gasp in wonder when he saw the flying boy and snowman on TV. The next morning I booked four tickets. For the fifth of January.

. . .

What I did for my boys never stopped. Now I have to give that all up? During those months and months after the wave, I clutched the side of my bed, reeling with this thought.

But how do I stop searching the Web with Vik for Galápagos tortoises? How do I stop talking with him about dinosaur birds? How do I give up on Malli's dreams of being a dancer? Or the one who puts on shows? I had only just been thinking I really must get on with teaching him to read and write, that Christmas card he made us in school said "To Mum and Bab."

Mum. I could hear them. "Isn't it true, Mum . . . In a minute, Mum . . . Oww, don't turn the TV off, Mum . . . My leg hurts, Mum." I wanted to scratch out that word: *Mum*.

The torment of wanting them when they came up close like this. I will kill myself soon. But until then, how do I tame my pain?

I need to prise them off me. But how?

I must stop remembering. I must keep them in a faraway place. The more I remember, the greater my agony. These thoughts stuttered in my mind. So I stopped talking about them, I wouldn't mouth my boys' names, I shoved away stories of them. Let them, let our life, become as unreal as that wave.

They had become muffled and distant then anyway. This happened in those first days after the wave. I couldn't find their faces, they quivered as in a heat haze. Even in my stupor I knew that details of them were dropping away from me like crumbs. Still, whenever they emerged, I panicked.

I must be more watchful, I told myself. I must shut them out.

I couldn't always keep this up. I'd find myself tracing their outlines on my bed, remembering their sizes and shapes. They were so real, these imprints, almost warm. I wanted to fix them on those sheets, pin them down.

But I must stop this. I must turn away from them.

*T*hey don't want me to drink. Some cheek, I fumed. My relatives, of all people, hark at them, they who are always reaching for the next Scotch. Over the years, whenever my parents and my aunts and uncles were invited to a dinner party where there'd be no alcohol, it was a family crisis. They'd complain for weeks beforehand. Oh, so difficult, functions like this. They'd plan to meet early that evening and have their fill. And now, some nerve. These same relatives were trying to stop *me* from drinking?

In those early weeks, each evening someone would try to tempt me with a glass of wine. Come on, just one. Or a brandy then. It will relax you, help you sleep. But I refused. I feared it would blur the truth of what had happened. I had to be vigilant. What if, even for one single moment, I thought nothing has changed, that no one is dead?

Then suddenly every evening I was drunk. Half a bottle of vodka down by six p.m., never mind that my stomach burned. Then wine, whiskey, whatever I could stumble around the house and seize. I'd swig from bottles, no time to get a glass.

Now everyone panicked. They locked away the bottles (after they'd had their fill). My aunt hid the keys. Our friend Sarah came from London and emptied whole bottles of Baileys down the sink. You cow, I thought, such waste. I'd be incensed and try to drink bottles of aftershave, perfume, it's got alcohol in it, right? Ugh, the taste, I smashed bottles against walls.

Each night I hoped to die from my frenzied drinking. And it diluted my terror of getting to sleep. I knew I had to wake up the next morning and relearn the truth all over again. Sometimes I would guzzle from a bottle on the balcony all night, which was silent but for the flutter of moths. I would plead into the darkness, where are they, bring them back. I rushed inside when the birds began to sing at first light, birds I had to escape. Or instead I'd say to the *kohas,* go on, ramp it up, screech my pain.

If I drank through the night, I didn't have to dream. Each night I dreamed of fleeing, of running from something, some nights it was water, some nights it was churning mud, other nights I didn't know what. In these dreams always one of them died. Then I'd wake to face my real nightmare.

With the alcohol I continued to take pills. Though my prescribed sleeping pills were rationed, this was Colombo, and I could go to the pharmacy around the corner, no prescription needed, and stock up. Zolpidem, Halcion, Seroquel. After my evening of drinking, I'd pop two pills, then another two, another four, four more, and two more again, in quick succession. Then a mug of gin. Then another pill, if I could raise my arm to reach for it. The next morning I couldn't move, I felt faint when I stood up. I'd be shivery, my blood pressure dropped. My friend Keshini would sit on my bed, hands clasped, and talk sternly about my abuse of central nervous system depressants, I couldn't go on doing this, my heart would stop. I looked at her blankly. Huh, getting all technical on me, I thought.

I liked mixing alcohol with the pills. It made me hallucinate. I watched plump black worms crawl out from the air conditioner and slide down the wall. Hundreds of them, as slowly they crawled. When I sat on the balcony, I could see a man in a white suit swinging from a tree. I chortled and pointed him out to my friends. They pretended not to be spooked. This was good. I felt crazy, and that's how I thought I should be. My world gone in an instant, I need to be insane.

Half-drunk and half-drugged, I would search the Internet for images of the wave. Of scenes of destruction. Of dead bodies, mortuaries, mass graves. The more horrifying, the better. I'd gape at these for hours. I wanted to make it all real now, but I had to be drunk to even try to do that. There was also a numbness in me, due not to drink but to a deeper deadness, that I thought was preventing me from being truly insane. I wanted to spear it with these images. I searched on and on, hoping something would shock me into madness.

I kept Googling ways of killing myself. I needed

to know how to do it successfully, I couldn't mess
it up. And each time I logged in to my laptop, I'd
think: my password is the only thing in my life that
hasn't changed. I remembered Steve's password, and
I wished I hadn't. It always was "rosebud" something. Rosebud.

Sometimes I'd panic, in my drugged-up state,
about something that seemed very important. Like
library books. What am I to do, we didn't return the
children's library books, I'd keep saying, as I paced,
or swayed, up and down the hall. Those books we
took out from the Poetry Library in the South Bank.
I'm never going back to London, I can't return those
books. I did relish this at times, having something
normal to worry about.

My friends took me on short trips away from
Colombo, hoping to restrain me a little. It didn't
always work. It was after plenty of vodka and tablets
that I made Lester walk miles on a dark deserted
beach one night. I knew a place where turtles came
ashore to lay their eggs, and I wanted to show him.
For more than an hour, I stumbled on that beach—I
blamed the terrain, it was not flat, small dunes—I
didn't admit that I suspected we were lost. Lester
had seen me with that bottle of vodka earlier in the
evening and was concerned. The previous night I'd
drunk so much that I'd vomited several times and
passed out, and he'd sat by my bed until morning,
worried I might choke in my sleep. He thought I

was about to repeat this tonight as well. "What are we doing here?" he kept saying. "There is no one around, it's too dark." Finally we did come upon a green turtle, her soft eggs dropped into the huge pit she'd dug in the sand. We weren't alone now, a couple of German tourists were watching too. I crawled quietly up to the turtle, peered into the pit, held an egg in my palm. It was warm. I thought this was magical. I made Lester have a look, but he'd had enough. "It's Friday night," he barked. "I could be in London, I could be down the pub. What am I doing on a godforsaken beach with some Germans, looking up a turtle's arse?"

Two

*S*omeone had removed the brass plate with my father's name on it from the gray front wall. It had his name etched in black italics. I sat in the passenger seat of my friend Mary-Anne's car, my eyes clinging to the holes in the wall where that brass plate was once nailed.

This had been my parents' home in Colombo for some thirty-five years, and my childhood home. For my sons it was their home in Sri Lanka. They were giddy with excitement when we visited every summer and Christmas. Vik took his first steps here, and Malli, when younger, called the house "Sri Lanka." And in our last year, 2004, when Steve and I had sabbaticals from our jobs and the four of us spent nine months in Colombo until September, this house was the hub of our children's lives.

This was where we were to return to on the afternoon of the twenty-sixth of December. My mother had already given Saroja, our cook, the menu for dinner. This was where they didn't come back to.

Now, six months after the wave, I dared to set eyes on this house.

I was wary as I sat in Mary-Anne's car, which was parked by our front wall. I didn't want to look around. I was afraid of seeing too much. But I couldn't help myself, I peeked.

Apart for the now nameless wall, the outside of the house had not changed. The tall iron gates still had spikes on top to keep burglars out. The rail on the balcony was white and safe. The mango tree I was parked under was the same mango tree that gave me an allergic reaction when it flowered, that sickly tree, dark blotches on its leaves. I noticed some small black stones on the driveway, and I remembered. Vik would juggle with these stones when he waited out here for the New Lanka Caterers van to come by selling *kimbula paan*—sugarcoated bread rolls shaped as crocodiles.

It was a humid, sticky afternoon, and Mary-Anne rolled down the car windows. From its perch on a nearby telephone post, a bulbul trilled. And I recalled the pair of red-vented bulbuls that nested in the lamp that hung in the car porch, just over the front wall. In the hollow of the glass lampshade, there would be a nest built with dried twigs and leaves and even a green drinking straw. The boys were spellbound by the arrival of fidgety chicks, still part covered in pale red shell. They watched the first flutter from that lamp many times, shooing off the mob of crows that rallied on the wall waiting for an unready chick to drop to the ground. Now I could see the two of them, placing a chair under the lamp to stand on and get a better look. Shoving each other off that chair. *My* turn now. *I* wanna see the baby bird. Get off.

A phone rang indoors. It made me shiver. It was the same phone, the same ring. From my father's study on the other side of this wall, the phone kept ringing, no one picked it up. Now I could hear my father push back his chair to go tell my mother that it is her sister calling, again. I could hear him open the door of his study. A bunch of keys always dangled on that door. They tapped against the door's glass panel when it was opened or shut. I could hear them jingle.

In the past months, I'd been unable to focus on the death of my parents. I'd held back thoughts of them, so utterly bewildered was I by the loss of my boys and Steve. Now, as I lingered outside this house, my parents emerged, a little.

Then I saw through the branches of the mango tree that the windows of the bedroom upstairs were closed. That was my bedroom when I was a child. Then Vik and Malli slept there when we visited. Getting them to bed in that room took forever. They'd call to my mother to plead for yet another fizzy drink, and she'd gladly oblige. They'd squabble, trying to stretch a too-small mosquito net over two adjacent beds, and argue about how dark the room should be. Vik wanted some light, Malli did not. He'd say, "Don't be scared, Vik. It's good when it's all really black. You can see your dreams better."

I looked away from that upstairs bedroom. I stared at the empty space on the wall where the nameplate used to be. They must be still in that room, surely. It's impossible they are not.

I didn't go inside. Mary-Anne squeezed my hand as she started up the car to drive off. And I remembered how, on our last morning here, the day we left for Yala, I'd woken before the boys and packed their Christmas presents in two red bags. Vik had written his name on those bags with a black marker pen, one of those permanent ones.

I went back to the house at night because I could not bear to step inside in daylight. The tall metal gates shut, not partly open as they used to be. All the rooms in darkness, windows closed. The house was hushed, shuddering in disbelief. A solitary light burned on the balcony, another in the car porch. I glanced quickly at the lamp in the porch, some scraps of a nest, no birds. The large wooden front door rumbled back on its rollers. I kept my sandals on as I walked in, not kicking them off by the tall, bronze-framed mirror on the wall below the stairs, as I used to.

As I walked through those front doors, the huge silence of the house ripped through me. I had tried to come inside here on many nights before but hadn't made it past the gates. Damn you, I kicked those metal gates, all those gin and tonics I'd knocked back powering my legs. Damn this house. Damn everything.

The house I entered was transformed, empty and vast, bereft. Just a few pieces of furniture remained, repositioned, displaced. The floors now bare, no rugs to absorb my footsteps. The walls gleamed with new paint that concealed even the impressions left by the mirrors, the paintings, and old blue and white porcelain plates that had been taken down.

I didn't want this barrenness. I yearned for the

house as it was, as we left it. I wanted to sit on every
couch, on every chair they sat on, and maybe some
warmth would seep into me. I wanted wardrobes
full of their clothes, a mixed-up mound of the boys'
underwear in ours, a neat stack of my father's white
handkerchiefs in his. I wished I could pick up a
book Vik had been reading from the table by our
bed, and turn to the page he'd folded to mark where
he had stopped. I wanted the green roll-on stick of
mosquito repellant on that table, drying out because
we had left the cap off. But none of this could be.
Broken and bewildered, my brother had the house
cleared and packed away, painted and polished, all
in the first month or two after the wave. For him,
that was the practical thing to do, to impose order
on the unfathomable, perhaps. I had been collapsed
on a bed in my aunt's house at the time and could
not contemplate returning to my parents' house. I
quaked at the very thought of it.

Now, in this stillness, sterile with the odor of
varnish and paint, I hunted traces of us. A pencil
stub with the end chewed off perhaps, a scrunched-
up grocery bill, a hair floating across the floor, a
squiggle made with a pen on a wall, a scrape of a
fork on a table. But there was nothing. No dent,
no chipped paint on the wooden banister along the
stairs where a ball had been lobbed too hard. The
drops of crimson nail polish on the white table in
my parents' bedroom had vanished. The chocolate

smears on the sofa bleached out. Surely this cannot be. There must be some atom of our life hidden here, lingering in this quiet somewhere.

And then I saw it. The mat. Just a small square black rubber mat with little round bristles, unremarkable. But I was transfixed. This was the mat Vik wiped his muddy feet on when he bounded in from the garden. The very same mat. It was inside the house now, tossed to the side by the stairs, not on the step leading out to the garden as it should be. No one had bothered to dispose of it, no one had bothered to clean it up. The gaps between the bristles were flecked with scraps of disintegrating dried grass, grains of sand, a morsel of dead beetle that the ants had tired of. Was that an imprint of Vikram's foot? Did that speck of dirt come off his heel? This mat and suddenly the house was not so lifeless, pulsing faintly, ever so slightly charged with their presence. I could almost hear them, turning the page of a book and shifting softly on a rattan armchair, crunching a roasted cashew nut and dropping another on the floor, slipping an ice cube into a glass and placing the tongs back on the table.

I walked into the hollow that had been my father's office. There was no large desk heaving with piles of legal briefs, those blue and beige folders frayed at the edges, sometimes tied up with a piece of thin ribbon. The wooden shelves that stretched from the floor to the ceiling on two walls were

bare, the top ones no longer warped by the weight
of too many books. No antique maps of Sri Lanka
hung above the desk. One of these maps, from the
sixteenth century, showed the island as a rectilinear
pentagon, not unlike a small child's lopsided drawing of a house, and in the middle, along with a few
mountains and rivers, the cartographer had etched a
colorful elephant with ornate anklets on all its feet,
perhaps to compensate for the lack of geographical
detail.

As I stood in the dark of that room, fragments of
our last days here kept flaring up, unbidden. Malli
tying clusters of balloons on the frangipani trees
in the back garden because we were having friends
to dinner, and what's a party without balloons. My
mother teaching Vikram to play "Silent Night" on
the piano, and his deliciously dimpled smile as he
changes the chords and presses hard on the pedal,
making the tune unrecognizable. Steve wearing that
burnt-orange shirt the night we had the party, the
shirt I'd bought him only that day, a tad more flam-
boyant than his usual choice. All of this now sharply
in focus just by being within these walls, my vapor-
filmed mind clearing for a while. I looked out the
window and saw the lime tree in the front garden.
The tangy smell of those lime leaves, when they are
torn into small pieces, I know that so well. Familiar
insect noises filled the outside, crickets rubbing

wings together, cicadas vibrating tiny abdominal membranes. A few moments of quiescence. Home.

Upstairs in our bedroom, the two double beds, no sheets or pillows, naked. The wardrobe empty, I traced inside the shelves with my fingers, and there was no dust. In the corner of a drawer, I found some seashells, small cowries that Malli and I gathered on the beach, feeling their pearly smoothness under our thumbs. He called them "favorites," both his and mine. Drifting in and out of the rooms in a daze, I looked into the small shrine room at the top of the stairs. On the floor, under the Buddha and Ganesh statues, was a set of Vikram's cricket stumps, the tallest ones he had, Steve would tap them into the ground with his bat in the middle of the athletics track of the Sports Ministry playing fields every evening. I picked up one of the stumps, staring at its pointed end that was darkened with soil, the wetness of the earth still clinging to the wood, almost. I took it to our bedroom. I struck at the bed. I stabbed the mattress with the muddied pointed end, over and over, harder and harder, until a tear appeared, and again to make the hole deeper and again to make another gash and again to join up all the gashes. The four of us, we slept here in all our innocence. That'll teach us.

*D*ust, rubble, shards of glass. This was the hotel. It had been flattened. There were no walls standing, it was as though they'd been sliced off the floors. Only those clay-tiled floors remained, large footprints of rooms, thin corridors stretching out in all directions. Fallen trees were everywhere, the surrounding forest had flown apart. As if there'd been a wildfire, all the trees were charred. A sign-board fallen in the dirt said YALA SAFARI BEACH HOTEL. I stumbled about this shattered landscape. I stubbed my toe on this ruin.

This was my first trip back to Yala. I went with Steve's father, Peter, and his sister Jane. On the two-hundred-mile drive from Colombo, we had to stop often, so I could vomit.

The wind was fierce that day we went back, it flung sand into our faces. A strangely quiet wind, though, bereft of the rustling and shaking of trees. It was midday, and no shelter from the seething sun. The sea eagles that had thrilled Vik, they were still there. Bold in this desolation, they sailed low, sudden shadows striking the bare ground. Eagles without Vik. I didn't look up.

I couldn't make this real. This wasteland. What has *this* got to do with me? I thought. *This* was where I was last with my family? Our wine chilled in a

bucket *here* on Christmas Eve? I couldn't believe any
of it, for I couldn't grasp their extinction.

I had learned some facts by now, so I recited
them in my head. The wave was more than thirty
feet high here. It moved through the land at twenty-
five miles an hour. It charged inland for more than
two miles, then went back into the ocean. All that I
saw around me had been submerged. I told myself
this over and over. Understanding nothing.

I knew the geography of this hotel so well—
but now I was directionless. Where do I go? What
did I come here to see? Then I remembered the
rock. There was a large rock here on the bank of
the lagoon that is to the side of the hotel. A black,
peaceful rock that we'd often sit on at dusk. Every
year we took photos of the boys on that rock. I had
to search awhile before I saw it now, it wasn't where
it used to be. It was in the middle of the lagoon. Had
it moved, or had the lagoon expanded? I couldn't
tell. But with that rock I found my bearings. These
concrete pillars held up the dining room. Over there,
behind that mound of crushed concrete, was the
pool. The rooms we stayed in were at the farthest
end, near to the jungle, and at night we heard wild
boar steal out of the scrub.

I showed Steve's father and sister those rooms.
They stared silently at the floor of the bathroom,
where Steve was when I saw the wave. I retraced the

path we took as we ran from the water. I showed them the driveway where we climbed into the jeep. We stood on that gravel awhile. I kicked up red dust.

I noticed objects wedged in the top branches of a large acacia, one of the few trees still upright. An air-conditioning unit, a pink mosquito net, the number plate of a car. And in the rubble on the ground, I could see a Japanese magazine now dried to a curl, a room-service menu, a broken wineglass, a black high-heeled shoe. A child's red underpants. My eyes rushed past this. I didn't want to find anything that was ours.

I walked down to the ocean alone. It was June, when the surf here is wild. I stared. These waves, this close. I stood there taunting the sea, our killer. Come on then. Why don't you rise now? Higher, higher. Swallow me up.

When I came back to my father-in-law, he was holding a sheet of paper, peering at it. He showed it to me. He told me he'd stood in that wind and spoken a few words into the air, to Steve and the boys. That's when something fluttered by his foot. He took no notice. It was just a scrap of paper, mostly covered in sand, some old newspaper, he thought. With each gust of wind, it kept flapping. So he dug it out. It was a laminated page, A4 size. Could this be something of Steve's? he asked.

I looked. And I looked. My blood jumped. For it was.

It was the back cover of a research report written by Steve and a colleague. A report on "using random assignment to evaluate employment programs," published in London in 2003. The ISSN number was still clear on the bottom left. Except for a small tear in the middle, this page was intact. It had survived the wave? And the monsoon in the months after? And this relentless wind? It appeared right by Steve's father's foot? It rustled? Random assignment. I remembered the many studies that Steve had been working on, these two words absurd in this madness now. Had Steve been reading this on the toilet when I shouted to him? Was this one of the last things touched by his hands? I clasped the paper to my chest and sobbed. My father-in-law stood next to me. "Cry all you want, sweetheart."

After finding that page, I was no longer afraid of chancing upon our belongings amid this rubble. Now I wanted to discover more. I kept going back to Yala, obsessively, over the next months. I scavenged the debris of the hotel. I searched, dug about, scratched my arms on rusted metal. I pounced on fragments of plastic, did this come from one of our toys? Is this Malli's sock? What I really wanted was to find Crazy Crow, the big glove puppet with unruly black feathers that we had given Malli for Christmas, the day before the wave. When he tore open the wrapping and saw it, how he'd lit up.

I followed the course of the wave inland, time and again. In a trance, I scrambled through the uprooted scrub. The jungle had been devoured by the water, vast tracts of it were now covered in bone-white sea sand that had been swept in by the wave. I ignored danger and walked far into the forest, there were wild animals—elephants, leopard, bear. I lied to my unsuspecting friends from London who sometimes came with me. "Are you *sure* this is safe?" "Yeah, course it is, come on."

Nothing was normal here, and that I liked. Here, in this ravaged landscape, I didn't have to shrink from everyday details that were no longer ours. The shop we bought hot bread from, a blue car, a basketball. My surroundings were as deformed as I was. I belonged here.

I kept returning over the next months and saw the jungle begin to revive. Fresh green shoots sneaked out from under crushed brick. New vines climbed around tilting pillars, and these ruins suddenly looked ancient, like some holy site, a monastery for forest monks, perhaps. Around our rooms a scattering of young *ranawara* bushes dripped yellow blossoms. And everywhere, on bare ground and between cracks in the floors, tiny pink and white flowers that flourish along the seashore forced their way up. *Mini mal*, or graveyard flowers, they are called. I resented this renewal. How dare you heal.

Still, I began to experience a new calm. In Colombo my chest cramped continuously, here that pain lessened. I lay on the warm floor of our hotel room as a slow moon scaled above the sea, and I could breathe. At the edge of this floor, there was a small bolt-hole, filled with sand. When I saw the wave coming toward us, I asked Vik to shut the back door. It was into this bolt-hole that he pulled down the lock. Now I traced its rim with my fingers. I cleaned out the sand.

We loved this wilderness. Now slowly it began pressing into me, enticing me to take notice, stirring me from my stupor, just a little. And here I found the nerve to remember. I'd walk on the beach following the footsteps of a solitary peacock, and allow in snatches of us. I could see Vik and Malli catching hermit crabs on this beach. They'd keep the crabs in a large blue basin that they'd landscaped with sand tunnels and ditches, then release them by the water's edge at the end of the day. Now I could hear the two of them, their innocence twinkling in the late-evening light. "Have I been good, Mum, and will Santa bring me lots of presents?"

I had glimpses of those hours before the wave. Vik jumped on my bed. "Come give me cuddle," I said. "A Boxing Day cuddle?" he asked, snuggling up. We were to check out of the hotel soon, my mother would have had her vanity case packed. I remembered our last night here, a star-sprawled sky. "Look, Dad, the sky has got chicken pox." We were sitting outside on the sand, the air was still, from the *mayila* trees, like a marble skipping on stone, a nightjar called. A fucking nightjar? When I needed a vast pronouncement, of what was looming. The end of my world.

I never did find Crazy Crow. I stopped searching the day I found the shirt Vik wore on our last evening, Christmas night. It was a lime-green cotton shirt. I remembered him fussing that he didn't want to wear it, it had long sleeves, which he didn't like. Steve rolled up the sleeves for him. "There, that looks smart." When I found the shirt, it was under a spiky bush, half-buried in sand. I pulled it out, not knowing what this piece of tattered yellowing fabric was. I dusted off the sand. Those parts of the shirt that had not been bleached by salt water and sun were still bright green. One of the sleeves was still rolled up.

*M*y journeys to Yala became less frequent after I began to harass the Dutch family. By that December, as the first anniversary of the wave approached, I had this new fixation. Strangers had moved into our home in Colombo. A Dutch family. When I was first told the house had been rented to them, I raged at Rajiv for doing it. I was desperate. I screamed. I explained: the house, it anchors me to my children. It tells me they were real. I need to curl up inside it, now and again. But my brother could not comprehend any of this. Why would I want to crawl back into that torturous space? It was so empty of them now. And he didn't live in Sri Lanka, and I was not in a state to manage it. He had no choice but to rent out the house.

But I smashed my head on the wooden frame of the bed after he told me this. Again and again I bit my arm.

I was spinning in a helpless rage. My boys have been flung out of their home. Other people are in our house, infesting it, erasing Vik and Mal. I want to sit in our garden. I want to pluck on a blade of grass that my boys pounded on. And I can't? All these months with everyone coaxing me, you have to live, and now I can't even do this?

On the night I learned about the Dutch family, I drove to our home. I went alone.

Wave

I know what I'll do, I thought. I will smash the car into the front wall. It will burst into flames. I will die. That will be fitting. Killing myself in our home. I'll do it with an explosion. I'll do it in style.

This was my first time driving alone since the wave. It was dusk, when traffic is cranky on Colombo roads. I tore through, steering with one hand, overtaking on the wrong side. I played one of Steve's old The Smiths CDs. My friends from England had brought me a selection of our music, but I couldn't bear to listen to most of it. I did play The Smiths, though. Hearing them didn't feel so raw, they were not from our immediate life. It was when we were undergraduates in Cambridge that Steve was possessed by them. Now, in the car, I played "There Is a Light That Never Goes Out" repeatedly. "And if a ten-ton truck kills the both of us, to die by your side, well the pleasure, the privilege is mine." Ah, this is noble. I swung the car into our street.

When I approached the house, my foot wouldn't slam on the accelerator pedal as I'd planned. I slowed down just as I did when we lived here. Just as then, I got to the front gates and stopped. The gates were closed. We always kept them ajar at this time, and our security guard would open them when I pulled up. He'd wake from his nap for the glare of the headlights and rush out in disarray, tripping over his open sandals, buttoning his shirt. None of that now. The gates stayed shut.

I could see curtains open in all the bedrooms.
Lights were on. Other children, in Vik and Malli's
room. Other children, readying for bed upstairs. It
is December. These other children, will they have a
Christmas tree? Will they put it right where we put
ours? My head dropped to the steering wheel.
I stayed a few minutes. Then drove off.

Strangers in our home. It's ghastly. The Dutch
family, settling in there like nothing's happened.
They must be dancing around in their fucking clogs.

I can't allow them to stay, I vowed. Our home is
sacred. I need to get it back. But how?

Maybe I can scare them. Hound them out.

So I went back, every night. "There Is a Light
That Never Goes Out" became my anthem. The
bounce in the music made me drive fast. And of
course the lyrics. Morrissey was singing for me.
"'Because it's not my home. It's their home. And
I'm welcome no more.'" I shouted along.

Powered by The Smiths and several shots of
vodka, I didn't sit outside the house silently anymore. I got out. I pounded on the gates. Those gates
are made of metal sheets, they boomed as I punched
and kicked. Hello, Dutch family. All nice and calm in
the house, is it? A peaceful Sunday evening? I'll show
you peaceful. Take this. When I heard the front
door open, I drove off. Then returned ten minutes
later, kicked the gates again. They must be getting
worried now, surely. Just a teeny bit. It's happening

every night. Some nutter banging on the gates at all hours. They must be unnerved. How much it pleased me, that thought.

Sometimes I'd ring the doorbell. At two a.m. Asleep, are we? Not for long, you won't be. I'll see to that. I had to keep my finger pressed on that button for many minutes before anyone stirred. No security guard ran to the gate in disarray. He must have taken Ambien, like me, I thought. A light would come on upstairs, in what was my parents' room, and I'd get back in the car and blare the horn. Or I'd wind down the car windows and turn the music up. More of The Smiths. "Bigmouth Strikes Again" now. I hope you can hear this in there, I said as the car stereo hammered out the words "by rights you should be bludgeoned in your bed" in our hushed Colombo street.

I drove back with a swagger along an empty Bullers Road. I laughed out loud.

I suddenly felt more in command, not so powerless. Steve will appreciate what I am doing, I thought. Scaring away the Dutch, this is taking some imagination. Steve will be pleased I've still got that.

Alone in the darkness of my car, I was able to let in thoughts of my family. For some moments at least, I didn't try to quell them. Ringing the doorbell reminded me of Steve's yarns about playing knock-down-ginger when he was a child roaming his East

London council estate during school holidays. He taught our boys to try the prank on me. If I was home when they returned from the park, they'd ring our bell and scram to hide behind the hedge next door: "Shh . . . Mummy doesn't know it's us." I could hear them now, as I drove through a red light at the Thunmulla junction. I shrank back from their voices. I couldn't see the road in front of me for wanting them.

Since I started on the Dutch family, my days livened up. I still woke paralyzed by the chant "they are dead," but slowly my mind revived. I had to plan for the night. I lay in bed and schemed. Getting rid of the Dutch required serious thought. I'll go to the house at different times each night, I won't be predictable. I'll give you a few nights' break, my lovely little tulips, and when you think it's all over, I'll start again.

I clasped a seashell in my fist as I strategized, one of those cowrie shells I found in the house before it was rented. On its shiny surface still, Malli's fingertips.

My relatives and friends became concerned about my nightly forays. After months of begging me to leave my room, they now tried to hide the car keys. "You mustn't harass those tenants, they are innocent in this, it's not their fault," they'd plead. "You are driving yourself insane."

Finally. I was insane. I liked this. And even if I

didn't really believe I was, I welcomed the chance
to act as if deranged. I'd been too compliant since
the wave, immobilized on that bed, crushed and
numb. Everyone's dead, that's not how I should be,
I should be raving around.

I began phoning the Dutch family. At night,
late. At first I had to force my fingers to tap out that
number. They hovered over the keypad as if incredulous that I wasn't calling my mother. The first few
times I called, I said nothing when the Dutch man
answered. "Who is this? Who *is* this?" he kept asking. A chilling silence from me, I thought. Let him
think this is a portent of worse to come.

It tore my skin off to hear a stranger speaking to
me from the phone in my parents' bedroom. When
Ma called me in London to ask if Malli's fever was
better or to check on how my biryani turned out,
she used that phone. I have to be more fierce. I have
to free our house.

I moved on to making sinister noises when the
phone was answered. I hissed, I rustled, I made
ghostly sounds. The Dutch man spoke with more
urgency now. "What is it you want?" he said time
and again. "Tell me, please. What is it you want?"

My phone calls made my relatives panic even
more. You will be arrested, they said. But Vik
and Mal will be so impressed by my ghostliness,
I thought. They loved being scary at Halloween.
The chords of my "hoo-ooo" were borrowed from

the low-pitched howl with which Vik caused gleeful dread among his friends at costume parties. In
the weeks before Halloween, our house in London
would tremble with bloodcurdling sounds. Now,
sitting in bed with the phone on my lap, I remembered how I'd thrilled the boys with my rendition
of Hamlet—" 'Tis now the very witching time of
night." I never got beyond "when churchyards yawn"
though, they squealed too much. I don't want to
think about them, I said to myself. I must focus
on the Dutch.

More than a month after I started on them, and
they still wouldn't leave. If this was happening to
Steve and me, we would have been out of there like a
shot, I thought. She's completely bonkers, we can't
take a chance, Steve would have said, if some woman
was stalking us night after night. Vik liked using the
word "bonkers," and I would scold him. He used it in
the poem about "Craziness" he'd written in school
in that last month. They must have been learning
about emotions. The poem began "Craziness is like
jelly beans jumping in your head" and ended "Craziness is bonkers and bonkers is the best."

Even when Steve's family arrived in Colombo for the
first anniversary of the wave, I refused to be distracted from my mission. We were having a memorial service in Colombo, and invitations had been

printed. I couldn't bring myself to even glance at the words on that invitation, but I took one and posted it to the Dutch. If they don't yet know why I am harassing them, now they will. Surely this will make them understand why they should not stay on in the house. We played The Smiths at the memorial service in the chapel of my old school, Ladies' College. Of course it had to be "There Is a Light That Never Goes Out." For Steve.

I didn't succeed in ousting the Dutch family. A couple of months into my terror campaign, they changed their phone number, *our* phone number. And after that first anniversary I began living my days once again in a haze of vodka and Ambien. I was back in my bed, no strength to stand up, let alone to drive a car and go gate-bashing. At times I was mad at Steve. Why don't *you* go to the house for a change, Steve. *You* can rattle their beds and yowl through the windows and send them packing. Having me do the dirty work as usual. Why do *I* have to be the fucking ghost?

Three

I was dizzy in that room. I felt faint with disbelief. I held on to the seat of my chair to stay upright. I knew what was going on, but I couldn't absorb any of it. This is London, I kept telling myself. Pall Mall. A room at the Royal Society. That's where I am. During the two hours I sat in that room, my eyes tried to dodge the screen in front of me. "Stephen Lissenburgh Memorial Lecture," it said. Steve?

It's over now, the lecture that Steve's research institute organized. I could only gaze vacantly at the speaker on the podium. I didn't hear many words. I was calm while chatting with that crowd at the reception after, though, had a glass of white wine, a quail egg. Maybe I didn't look stunned.

Now I am with friends at a bar near the Royal Society, the ICA bar. It was my idea to come here. I suggested it, not stopping to think that this is somewhere Steve and I often came.

I am in England? I can't grasp the truth of this. This is the first time I've come back to England, and it is now almost two years since the wave. But

the reality of being here eludes me, I can't focus,
I am dazed. And I want to stay this way. If I have
too much clarity, I will be undone, I fear. I was in a
panic when I walked up Piccadilly on the way to the
lecture this evening. I didn't look around, wanting
to somehow disregard my familiar surroundings. I
am only staying a couple of nights, I reassure myself,
I won't even notice I've been back. And our home
in North London, even the thought horrifies me, I
won't be going anywhere near it.

But I am at the ICA bar? I don't want to know
this. Steve and I would come here before going to a
movie at the Curzon Soho. We'd have a drink here
first and stroll up Regent Street. At the cinema, Steve
always had a black coffee, I had a ginger and honey
ice cream. Now I stop these thoughts. Because I am
about to say, No we don't have time for another
drink. The film starts at seven. Let's get a move on,
Steve.

ENGLISH COUNTRYSIDE, 2007

*I*t was the light that did it. It was the angle of the sun at five o'clock on a Sunday evening in early March on a country road somewhere in Shropshire. It was those sinking rays slanting against a yew tree and glinting on the wing mirror on my side of the car, dazzling my eyes. The hawthorn hedgerows on either side of the road throw long shadows in this light. This light that is so very familiar unexpectedly makes me forget. It makes me forget that I am driving back from Wales with my friends David and Carole. It sends me into our car, Steve at the wheel, the boys at the back. The four of us drive the gentle curves of an English country road as we have done innumerable times before.

For three years I've tried to indelibly imprint *they are dead* on my consciousness, afraid of slipping up and forgetting, of thinking they are alive. Coming out of that lapse, however momentary, will be more harrowing than the constant knowing, surely. But now I am unmoored simply by the familiar light. This is different from remembering them, warily, as I usually do. This is tumbling into them, into our life, into our car. This is slipping up. I can see the tiny starlike crack on the windscreen made by the pebble that shot out of the road and smashed into

the glass no sooner than we'd bought the car. The
AA road atlas by my feet is trodden and creased.
Vik sits behind me, Malli behind Steve. There are
two Ribena cartons between them, drained empty
so their sides are curved in, the last drops of black
currant juice leaking out the straws and staining the
seat. Also, a spit-covered core of an apple that one
of them could easily have thrown out the window
instead of leaving there to roll off and rot under the
accelerator pedal. We have to get home and fix their
dinner. The rush of Sunday evenings.

Was that a dead pheasant on the side of the
road? They are not here, they would have noticed
it if they were. They would have said something.
Yuk. Cool. When do you think it got killed, Dad?
They are not here. But I don't want to emerge out
of them. I want to hover inside our metallic blue
Renault Mégane Scénic. Why am I allowing this? I
will have to crawl back into reality soon, and that
will be agony. Maybe it is the somnolent warmth of
Dave's car that entices me to forget in this way. Now
I slip up again, this time voluntarily.

They are sitting quietly at the back, not kicking
each other's shins for a change, no burping contests.
Vik sees a gush of starlings wing the air, his eyes trail
the whirr of gray filling the sky. But what he really
wants to see is a sparrow hawk. Or, better still, a
sparrow hawk sparring with a crow. Malli's nodding
off, he always does this in the car, but it's too late

to nap now. "Vik, talk to Malli and keep him awake, sweetheart. He won't sleep tonight if he dozes off now." They will run up the stairs to our front door and keep ringing the doorbell even though they know there is no one in. They will fight about whose turn it is to pee first. Steve will suggest that all three of them pee together, and they will do so gleefully. I will ask why one of them can't use the other toilet upstairs. And I will tell them not to spray the whole bloody place. When they are done, they will use the blue and white hand towel to mop up the floor a little and then hang the towel back on the rail. I will hear their giggles over the gulping and gurgling of the flush. But that's when we get home. We are still in the car, and the boys are both sitting in their socks because Steve has flung their muddy shoes into the boot.

Malli is proud of his new hiking shoes, brown Timberlands with thick soles, just like Daddy's shoes. He didn't complain and ask to be carried when we walked in the woods today. You have the best shoes, Mal, you lead the way, we told him. He said the small red tags on the back of his shoes glowed like lights and that would stop us getting lost, even on the darkest paths. He set off in front with a purposeful tread, stopping only to test the grip of his soles on an uneven slope or to pick blackberries. The berries were scarce today, the bushes on our path offered only dried-up brown clusters speckled with a few tiny purple beads, which the boys painstakingly picked out and then winced at their sourness when they crushed them between their teeth. Vik stepped on some nettles, and Steve showed him how to rub a dock leaf on his leg to stop the stinging. You always find dock leaves near nettles, he told Vik. We walked a long way today, and Malli didn't want to turn back once, simply because of his new shoes.

And then I remember. Shoes. Those shoes. I remember those shoes, and my heart shivers. The police took away one of those shoes from my parents' house when they were trying to identify bodies. They took it for DNA testing. They returned it in a sealed polythene bag, like a large sandwich bag. I am beaten. The one time I allow my family to come alive, and that shoe trounces me. But I want to linger with them. I want to stay in our car forever. Let's put the boys to bed early and watch *The Catherine Tate Show,* I say to Steve. I have to plan my lecture for tomorrow morning, but that can wait. What am I on about? *The Catherine Tate Show?* It wasn't even on then. That was after our time, we missed all that. Now I have to surrender, I have to squirm back into reality. But daylight is collapsing fast, and the air outside is sharpening, as it always does in early spring. And I can hear a voice from the back of the car say, *Is it a school day tomorrow, Mum?* And if I turn around . . .

Four

*I*t's a piece of pyrite. Fool's Gold, they call it, but Vikram always insisted on its proper name. He'd looked it up in his book on rocks and minerals. This small glistening nugget is right where Vik had left it nearly four years ago. On the mantelpiece in the playroom. I pick it up, and I remember. He bought it at the Science Museum. It was our last weekend in London. You can spend two pounds, we told him, and that's what he chose. My eyes cannot focus on any one thing in this playroom, but the Fool's Gold, this I can see. And the two red schoolbags, hanging on the door handle as always. I pick up the rock and press it tight into my palm. But I can't touch those schoolbags, each one now a scalpel.

This is moments after all the wailing in the hallway. Once Anita shut the front door behind us, I was a howling heap on the floor by the stairs. So I had finally done it. I had stepped into our home for the first time since I walked out of there with Steve and the boys that early December evening. Three years and eight months ago, almost to the

day. And through much of this time I could think
of our home only with dread and fear. In those early
months, when I could not lift myself off that bed, I
wished it destroyed. I wanted all traces of it erased.
Then later I needed the assurance that it was there
for me, preserved as we left it. But its existence also
tormented me. I shrank away from any talk of it. I
shuddered at the thought of seeing it. I couldn't go
back. Even a peek into the house would dismember
me even more than I already was, surely. Hollow and
barren, that's what it would now be, our home. But
when I finally stopped shaking and heaving in that
hallway and leaned back on the banister to catch
my breath, my eyes rested on the ceiling, and I was
startled. It didn't seem like we'd been gone at all.
That cornicing up there, I'd seen it this morning
surely, when the boys came down the stairs, when
the mirror on the opposite wall held their faces for
just one moment as they leaped off the fifth or sixth
step.

Now I walk into every room, sit on the floor. The
house is much as we left it. Here is our debris, but
it is all intact. All of it. I am bewildered. I can't join
the pieces together. They are dead, my life ruptured,
but in here it feels as it always did. They could have
walked out ten minutes ago. This house has not lost
its rhythm, it doesn't need reviving. During the
past four years, our life here often seemed unreal,
vaporous, and maddeningly elusive. But now it

emerges and breathes into me slowly from within these walls.

In these years I have only seen a few of our belongings. Friends from London brought a few things to Colombo for me in those early months. Some framed photographs that I couldn't bear to look at, a T-shirt of Steve's that I wear at night and that is now threadbare, *Clifford the Big Red Dog,* which I hid away. And now here is everything. A swirl of images dazes me. I can grasp but a handful.

There is, of course, the evidence of our absence and of when it all ended. The branches of the two apple trees now spread across the width of the garden, we would have pruned them. When I went to the foot of the garden earlier, a startled fox leaped into the neighbor's lawn through a hole in our fence but kept staring at me, now an invader in its territory. The yellowed *Guardian* newspapers in the rack in the living room are from the first week of December 2004. Stuck on the wall of our study is a printout of four tickets for *The Snowman* at the Peacock Theatre on the fifth of January 2005.

There is a pile of unopened Christmas presents on our bedroom floor. I remember now. The presents were given to Vik and Malli by Steve's family the weekend before we left for Sri Lanka. "You'll get so many presents in Colombo," I told the boys. "It'll be more fun to open these when we get back." I find a Christmas card sealed in a red envelope, written by Vik to my parents. "To Aachchi and Seeya, we are coming to Colombo on the 8th of December, from Vikram and Malli." I must have forgotten to post it before we left. And a calendar for 2005 that Malli made in school, with a delicate design of orange and gold dots that he had crafted with a little boy's devotion. I am in shreds.

But as I drift tentatively around the house, an undertow of calm also tugs at me, drawing me away from the agony, just a little. I can almost slip into thinking that nothing has changed. That we still live here. In the playroom, Malli's baby doll sits in a stroller as always. His silver tiara is on the mantelpiece and, by the fireplace, his pink ballet shoes. On the floor, a few sheets of A4 on which Vik has written out the score charts of his imaginary cricket matches, Australia v Namibia, Zimbabwe v India, and of course to annoy me, Sri Lanka always lost. The little cloth badge he got for completing his eight-hundred-meter swim just a few days before we left London is on his bookcase. I said I would sew it onto his swimming shorts when we returned. On their wooden blue desk is a poem that Malli and I wrote about a purple-eared creature he named the Giddymeenony, who lived beyond the sea and had a cactus growing on its nose. With a drawing of it and all. In this playroom, they were so secure.

The boys' shoes are by the kitchen door, dried mud on them still. There is even some onion peel in that clay pot Steve used for cooking beef curry. A shaft of afternoon sun falls across the red sofa in the living room and, as always, I can see dust drifting in the beam. On the floor by the fireplace is the large bronze pot I bought in Cambodia. Malli once did a pee in it. I put my hand inside and pull out some black chess pieces. Upstairs in our study, a dead wasp on the floor, and another wobbling on the curtains, there was always a nest outside this window, and Steve and I were stung a few times. In the boys' bedroom, a medicine spoon that looks like it was used last night, with crystals of Nurofen syrup. On our bed a few hairs, not mine, Steve's and maybe Vik's. Two dinosaur-shaped toothbrushes in the bathroom, and a basket of laundry, Steve's sarong on the top.

I want to put them back in here, I just want to put them back. They would so want to be here, they loved this house.

This is exactly how I know our home to be. And now I find myself at ease. It feels natural, despite my protestations to myself that this is not ordinary or natural because they are not here and will never be. Before coming back here, I expected to be assailed by objects that I'd forgotten. But there are no surprises. I brace myself and open the wardrobes upstairs. Do I dare look at their clothes? Something is going to get me now surely. Cautiously, I open door after door and drawer after drawer. But it is all as I know it to be. There is not one sock that I pull out and think, I don't remember this one. And after all the rummaging, my eyes cling to a white school shirt of Vik's, all washed and ironed, waiting patiently on its hanger. He wore this to his school Christmas concert the night before we left London. I hesitate, then take the shirt off its hanger and hold it, feeling its softness. None of this so menacing now.

How I relished my time alone at home back then, on those days when I was meant to be working from home and the boys were at school and Steve at the office. I would wander the house, put out the washing, make some tea, and maybe look out for the woodpecker that hammered holes in our garden shed. And here I am now, after our life ended, sitting on the floor of our living room, leaning against the sofa and staring at the tops of those overgrown apple trees with that same tranquillity stealing up on me. And I slip into my old ways, unthinkingly.

I begin tidying up a bit, putting things where they should be, or where *I* always thought they should be. What's Vik's cricket bat doing on the mound of soft toys? I pick it up and stand it by the box with the balls and bails, that is its rightful place. And Malli's puppets go with his dressing-up stuff. There is a bath mat by the radiator, I put it down by the shower. This laundry is clean, I should fold it. I carry the basket to the boys' room. And then I stop myself. What am I doing? Who am I readying the house for, they are not coming back. Don't be a fool, this is mad.

But I can't stop. I go into the kitchen and switch on the fridge. It doesn't feel right without that hum. I boil the kettle for no reason. On the draining board by the sink are two thin wooden placemats, Steve and I would have used them at dinner on our last night in the house. I wipe them and stack them on the shelf. And I pick up a small faded blue plastic bowl that's on the kitchen table. Anita and I found this in the middle of the lawn when I first walked into the garden earlier in the day. I recognized it in an instant then. It was the bowl that Vik ate his first solid food from when he was a few months old, one spoon of baby rice mixed in water. It must have become a garden toy over the years, we wouldn't have given it a second thought. Anita was surprised to see that bowl on the lawn. It wasn't here last evening, she insisted, she'd walked in the garden after the gardener cut the grass yesterday. So it must have been the foxes that brought it out later at night, then.

I stare at this little dirt-covered bowl, remembering Vik kicking his legs as he spat out his first mouthful of food. And I don't rush outside to put it away where it belongs, in the shed with the rest of the garden toys. It wouldn't be mad or foolish to keep it indoors now.

*S*arah, Niru, Fionnuala, and I sit around my
kitchen table. It is a dull autumn afternoon,
the sun punctures the gray now and then. We drink
tea and nibble dark chocolate, maybe expecting it
to revive us a little. We are still shaken. An hour
ago, when they each rang the doorbell and I opened
the door to them, we couldn't stop sobbing. We are
together in my home in London after nearly four
years.

And this is what we did so often. Back then. Our
children had been constants in each other's lives,
ever since Noah and Alex and Finian and Vikram
were a year old maybe, ever since we wheeled them
to our local library for story time. And over the
years, as our children went through school together,
the four of us would gather regularly to catch up
on our news—about work, about home, about the
play Sarah and I saw at the Donmar that week.
There would sometimes be a whirl of children about
us, sometimes not. Those precious school hours I
should have dedicated to that paper on the macro-
economic policy in Nepal were readily sacrificed for
a good gossip.

Now we are in this same kitchen, after it has all
ended. This is something I was sure we'd never do
again. Even when I decided to make a second visit
to our home and stay a few days, this was not part

of the plan. It would be too awful, it would be too familiar, and that would be unbearable, I thought. But I'd only been back some hours when I called my friends over. And then I panicked. This will be different from when we've previously met up in London in these last four years. Those surroundings—the café at Foyles bookshop, that Turkish restaurant in St. John's Wood—kept reality at bay, somewhat. But here in my home, I will be destroyed by getting too close to the life I lost.

And I was right. We sit here, and I lapse into thinking that nothing has changed, no one has died. It is one of those afternoons when Fionnuala and I take our sons to their football class in that sports hall, which, for some strange reason, we have to enter through a locker room full of partially clothed young men who've just played basketball, not that we complain. Then I have to remind myself. That life is over. But how can it be? Sitting here, that seems impossible. The steam from this kettle rises and drifts towards the window above the sink, just as it always did. That tap still drips if I don't give it an extra twist. The boys' mud-covered shoes are reassuringly by the kitchen door, they could have just come inside. And the green and pink marks on this kitchen table from Malli's colored pens are as bright as jelly beans.

My friends find the house calm and inviting, no different from before. They were nervous coming back here, not knowing how they'd react. For years now, they have looked away whenever they drove past our street. Today Niru was jolted by the sight of the garden, flashes of the boys' birthday parties we had there. Now we eat more chocolate and talk about those parties. We laugh, remembering Vik booting a ball through the window next door. We were sitting right here when we heard that shattering of glass.

We laugh, and I am unsettled. Why do I feel this lightness? This is indeed like the old times, but it seems bearable, I am enjoying it even. Then I warn myself. I shouldn't get too comfortable. Don't I know that Malli will not stand on that chair again, wearing a pink tutu and licking cake mix off a wooden spoon? Steve will not come in the front door at seven, there will be no clatter as he empties his pockets onto the table in the hall. The windows next door will remain intact. Still, I am relieved to reenter the warmth of our life, even though I know that reality will get me, later.

And right enough, it does. In the evening, the hush in this house is intolerable. I turn up the music, I talk loudly to Sarah, who is staying over, but this silence keeps ricocheting off the walls. I find myself listening out for the boys and Steve. There is a box of half-eaten chocolates on a shelf in the guest room. I can almost hear Vik and my mother whispering in that bed at night as they tuck into those chocolates, Ma ignoring my protests that the boy has already brushed his teeth. I am stunned by the quiet in the playroom. I turn on the light and see some star-shaped tinsel glistening on the floor, an entire galaxy at my feet.

When I lie in our bed the power of their absence assails me. The sheets have not been changed since Steve and I last slept on them. I haven't been able to bring myself to wash them, and so I sneeze all night. Steve's sarong still hangs on the exercise bike by the window. But his shoulder is not under my head. On Steve's pillow, the one his head hasn't touched in nearly four years, there is an eyelash.

I can't look, I pull the quilt over my face, yet I can see the four of us, crowded into this bed early on a Sunday morning. The boys have tiptoed into the room to announce at the tops of their voices that it is a sunny day. When I ignore them, Malli asks, "Why do humans need to sleep so much?" *Humans* was his word for adults, and we didn't correct him, just added it to that set of garbled words that was only ours. Now those words hover in this room, unuttered. And I am alarmed, not wanting to reawaken these memories, not here at night in so much quiet. I am now thankful for these dusty sheets, at least I have my sneezing to distract me.

In the morning I hear the squeak of floorboards. It is Sarah, already awake. I would get annoyed when Steve creaked about at six a.m. as he went between the bathroom and the study, turning on the computer, checking the NBA results from the previous night. I'd have thought this sound would unnerve me now, but this morning I find myself clinging to its familiarity, which soothes me somehow.

It is early light, and I step into the garden. Walking barefoot on dew-sodden grass, I always loved this. Autumn is the spider season, and the shrubs are aglitter with webs. Steve and the boys would feed the spiders. They'd carefully place a live ant on these silken threads and marvel as the spider trapped it between its legs and squeezed it into pulp. "See, it sucks up the ant juice like a milkshake," Steve told the boys. If there was an especially elaborate web, they'd implore me not to destroy it when I watered the garden.

And there is a lovely web on the climbing rose this morning, very showy and intricate. But they can't see it. So is it because I am hazy from sleep that I still feel a stab of wonder when I do? My desolation of last night is now dissolving, but is this just the cheer of the early sun? I wonder, but I am also certain that, for some time at least, I will keep returning to this house and to its warmth and comfort. There is a small snail edging across the table on the patio. The heat from its tiny body is thawing out the beads of frost that have studded the table overnight. It leaves a watery trail. They would be so stirred by this.

Five

I cower in a corner of my bed. I can barely raise my head. My stomach is clenched, my heart races, my right hand grips my left arm so tight it hurts. I shake all over, or at least it feels that way. Imagine if they could see me. They would be inconsolable.

I stay indoors alone for days on end in my apartment in New York, where I have been living these past few months. I can't face the sudden wintry brightness in this new city. I can't tolerate the happy scatter of children coming out of school. I can't bear a dimple on a small boy's cheek. Bloody hell, Steve, I sob into my pillow, how useless are you, wherever you are, why can't you sort this out. Just get me killed, I've more than had enough.

I am as I was in those early months when I was collapsed on a bed in my aunt's house in Colombo. But it's four years later now, and I am startled by the intensity of this fear in me. It came upon me all at once, when I was at our home in London recently, in late October. I felt one night, with a new and terrifying force, the way in which I was flung out of our life, just like that.

It was blustery, that night when I rifled through

some papers on Steve's desk. The windows behind me trembled, I could feel a draft on my back. Our office was tidier than it used to be, but the computer screen was tilted as always, so that in the daytime the branches of the silver maple that spread outside the window wouldn't reflect onto it and make you squint. I always had Jazz FM turned up loud when I worked in that room. But that night there was no music, only the wind.

The desk was piled up with Steve's usual stuff. Pages and pages of econometric models with some coefficients circled in blue ink, a book on chess, the *Wisden Cricketers' Almanack,* an appointment card for a haircut. I thumbed through Steve's checkbook, which was in the drawer. He'd written three checks on our last day in London, for the gardener and the milkman and for the boys' school dinners. Those two words, school dinners, were all it took. I shattered.

For one thing, my mind had not even murmured those words in all these years. How could I have forgotten? How could I have shut this out? I could now hear our daily conversations. Vik telling me that he'd had sausages again at lunchtime, Malli shrugging his shoulders and walking away when I ask if he's eaten any vegetables. And I could see Steve sitting right where I was, signing that check with the pen that is still on the desk, tearing it off and putting it in Vik's schoolbag. I would have seen that dinner bill lying around for days and left it for him to deal with. I would have picked it up when I sat at that desk reading a chapter of a student's thesis, stopping too frequently to read a film review on the *Guardian* website or to gaze at a shaft of late sun firing the red-brick chimneystacks of the houses across the street.

But it was not simply that I had forgotten about something as commonplace as school dinners that got me that night. As I stared at the stub in Steve's checkbook, I was held for a few moments in the coherence and safety of the life we had, when so much seemed predictable, when continuity was assumed. There would be more bills for Steve to sort out, more sunsets for me to get distracted by while he did just that. And as the wind gusted against those windows, I saw how, in an instant, I lost my shelter. This truth had hardly escaped me until then, far from it, but the clarity of that moment was overwhelming. And I am still shaking.

They would indeed be aghast to see the mess I am now. This is not me, this is not who I was with them. I can see that me as we left London for Colombo exactly four years ago today, the eighth of December, the day Steve wrote that check and we flew out of Heathrow's Terminal Four. Things couldn't have been better. I had it sorted. Steve and I were impatient for the three days we would spend in a small hotel on the coast, leaving the boys to be indulged by their grandparents. We'd have the room with enormous windows that open to the ocean on

three sides so the din of quickening waves smash-
ing against rock even enters your dreams. Then the
four of us and my parents would go to Yala, where
the soundless feet of a baby elephant hiding under
its mother's belly as she brushes past our jeep would
enthrall the boys. Steve and I were grateful our kids
didn't want to go Disneyland.

None of that assurance now as I shudder on
this bed. I recoil at my desolation. How I have fallen.
When I had them, they were my pride, and now that
I've lost them, I am full of shame. I was doomed all
along, I am marked, there must be something very
wrong about me. These were my constant thoughts
in those early months. Why else did we have to be
right there just when the wave hit? Why else have I
become this shocking story, this wild statistical out-
lier? Or I speculated that I must have been a mass
murderer in a previous life, I was paying for that
now. And even as I have discounted such possibilities over time, shame remains huge in me.

It is nearing Christmas, and I can't join in my
boys' giddy enthusiasm. I don't have my boys at the
kitchen table writing Christmas cards to kids they've
not spoken to all year or making greedy lists for
Santa. I can't do all those things that were normal
for us and still are for countless others. And I balk
at the failure that I am. Quite separate, this, from
the more obvious agony of missing them.

So I avert my eyes from the Christmas displays

in the shop windows on Bleecker Street because I don't have Malli here to be spellbound by them. Our last December I lifted him up in the London drizzle so he could see the tinkling *Nutcracker* exhibits outside Fortnum & Mason. But my arms are empty now, luckless mother that I am. I cross the street to avoid the smell of Christmas trees lined up for sale on the pavement near my apartment. Yet I remember our local Christmas-tree seller on Friern Barnet Road who wears a Santa hat as he does a roaring trade. One year he also sold us a red metal stand for our tree. "This is heavy duty, it'll last you forever, darlin'," he told me. I saw that red stand recently, it's still in our garden shed. I was conned. It wobbles.

It seems shallow, my shame, all about being trounced and not having, but that's how it is, and it won't dislodge. My time at home in London on that visit was tinged with it. I looked in the boys' wardrobes. They would have grown out of those clothes by now, I thought, and this felt like my defeat. It was half-term that week, and the tumble of children on trampolines filled neighboring gardens. I only had the silence indoors. So this is me now, loitering on the outskirts of the life we had.

In Colombo, there is no home now, not even one empty of them. I want the solace of that space, and I feel dispossessed. When I go back there, I break into a cold sweat and become nauseated as I pass through our neighborhood. It is unacceptable that I can't drive through those gates and walk into my child-hood home. I know every pothole on that street, my foot goes down on the clutch, and my hand changes gear with effortless recall. My memory of the house is immaculate. But I feel expelled from there. I lost my dignity when I lost them, I keep thinking.

I am in the unthinkable situation that people cannot bear to contemplate. I hear this occasionally. A friend will say, I told someone about you, and she couldn't believe it was true, couldn't imagine how you must be. And I cringe to be bereft in a way that cannot be imagined, even though I do wonder how impossible this really is. Occasionally an insensitive relative might walk away if I mention my anguish, and I reel from the humiliation of my pain being outlandish, not palatable to others.

Such a puny life. Starved of their loveliness, I feel shrunken. Diminished and faded, without their sustenance, their beauty, their smiles. Nothing like how I was that day before the wave, when we sat in the back of a jeep and watched a young male leopard leaping across the branches of a *palu* tree, supremely poised and scornful of the troop of monkeys that taunted him from the surrounding canopy. And nearby a haze of blue-tailed bee-eaters drifted in dust-filled light. Sometimes, even now, I can summon the lift of those birds. For some moments it takes me away from my fear and my shame.

*T*he woman next to me on the plane asks questions. I give her the briefest of answers. I pretend to sleep, it's been two long flights, from New York to Colombo. But the woman doesn't stop. "Do you have children?" "No." "Are you married?" "No." "Oh, it is good to be so dedicated to your career, no? You must be such a clever girl." Girl? And I haven't told her anything about a job. I smile politely. Why doesn't she get it that I don't want to speak with her? I haven't shown a modicum of interest in her life. "Do your parents live in Colombo?" "Hmm." I pretend to nod off again. We begin our descent over the Indian Ocean. She is even more animated. "Ooh ooh you'll be home for Christmas. You'll have a nice family Christmas, no? How nice." By now I can only muster up a feeble half-smile. "So what does your family do for Christmas? Big celebrations?" Oh shut up, you nosy cow, I think. You will probably faint if I tell you. You'll have to pull down your oxygen mask.

I steer clear of telling. I can't come out with it. The outlandish truth of me. How can I reveal this to someone innocent and unsuspecting? With those who know "my story," I talk freely about us, Steve, our children, my parents, about the wave. But with others I keep it hidden, the truth. I keep it under wraps because I don't want to shock or make anyone distressed.

But it's not like me to be cagey in my interactions. Steve and Vik would smirk and raise their eyebrows when I stopped to chat with yet someone else at the farmers' market or on Muswell Hill High Street. (Do you know *her* too?) But now I try to keep a distance from those who are innocent of my reality. At best I am vague. I feel deceitful at times. But I can't just drop it on someone, I feel—it's too horrifying, too huge.

It's not that I should be honest with everyone, the white lies I tell strangers I don't mind. But there are those I see time and again, have drinks with, share jokes, and even they don't know. They see my cheery side. And I kick myself for being a fraud. I don't even reveal half the story, about my parents, or Steve. Who knows where that might lead.

I think I also don't confess because I am still so unbelieving of what happened. I am still aghast. I stun myself each time I retell the truth to myself, let alone to someone else. So I am evasive in order to spare myself. I imagine saying those words— "My family, they are all dead, in an instant they vanished"—and I reel.

I can see, though, that my secrecy does me no favors. It probably makes worse my sense of being outlandish. It confirms to me that it might be abhorrent, my story, or that few can relate to it.

I have coffee with a friend who must think he knows me quite well. To him I am here in New York only to do research at Columbia, as I have a sabbatical from SOAS, my university in London. I am a carefree academic, he thinks. As we chat, I find I almost believe this story myself, so deft have I become at my trickery. This is mad, my pretense. I must come out with it. Now it's on the tip of my tongue, but I push it back.

Wave

I was out of tea bags this morning. Bleary-eyed, I stared into a red carton of Twinings English Breakfast Tea convinced it hadn't been empty last night. I rummaged in the cupboards for another box with no luck. There were plenty of other teas, oolong and jasmine and chamomile and that Japanese tea with toasted brown rice, but how can I drink that stuff in the morning? This would *not* have happened before, I griped. At home, we never ran out of tea. Or if I opened the tea caddy only to find a scattering of fragrant dust at the bottom, Steve would pop out to the shops for me. He'd be back in flash. He knows I can't think straight until I've had my two large cups first thing. This morning I crushed that empty carton and flung it into the bin. What am I supposed to do now, go out and get some tea bags? Unwilling to give in to the reality of having to do what Steve always did, I refused to take myself to the grocery shop on Eighth Avenue, even though it's just minutes away. So I put the kettle on and poured myself a mug of boiling water that I sipped in a sulk. How am I supposed to live without them?

Steve took the boys shopping, usually on Sunday afternoons. In those first weeks after the wave when my mind couldn't find their faces, one image that came to me was of the three of them returning from the supermarket, the boys squabbling over some sugary treat. And now today is a Sunday, and if they'd gone shopping, Vik would have claimed more than his fair share of sweets because this week is his birthday. He would have been twelve.

This time twelve years ago, Steve and I were impatient for Vik to be born. The hyperactive boy was making my belly swing from side to side with no letup, and thrilling as this was in the earlier months, it exhausted me. And I hated being crusty with the calamine lotion that soothed the prickly rash that covered my body in those last weeks. My parents were with us in London, excited, it was their first grandchild. Ma kept telling Steve that he needed to note the exact time of birth, to the minute or second even, her astrologer in Colombo couldn't write an accurate horoscope with approximate times.

Vik was born by emergency cesarean section, a sudden rush of midwives and doctors and needles in my spine, when I had only gone to the hospital for a routine checkup and his heartbeat was found to be alarmingly slow. Steve hid well from me the panic he later confessed to feeling then, but I had been unperturbed. That monitoring machine must be dodgy, I thought—nothing will go wrong now surely. And as the surgeon tugged and yanked about, I began to shiver with cold, the anesthetic they said. Steve warmed my hands in his, remembering all the while to glance at his watch. "Lots of hair," Steve said even before Vik was taken out, and moments

later, we both felt the magic of that soft black hair
in our hands.

The boys would trace the scar on my stomach
with their fingers, astonished they'd emerged from
there. This prompted Malli to want to be a mummy,
his doll wrapped in a wad of small blankets protrud-
ing from under his T-shirt, Vik's protests that boys
can't have babies resolutely ignored. It was calm
at the Royal Free Hospital when Malli was born, a
planned cesarean with no frantic dashing around,
but Steve forgot to check his watch. A few minutes
after noon, he mumbled to Ma, far too imprecise
for her astrologer's charts. Two-year-old Vik stared
awhile at his newborn brother and whispered,
"Malli," in a voice so tender that it still stirs my
heart. *Malli* means "little brother" in Sinhala, and we
always called him that, even though his given name
was Nikhil.

I can see us now, on the day he was born. What
bliss. Malli asleep on me. Vik, who was quickly bored
by his brother, clambering precariously onto the
handrail of my bed to look at a crane hoisting some
steel rods outside the hospital. Steve too elated to
worry the boy might fall. A Voltaren suppository
nicely numbing the pain of my cut. I think of that
day now, and I cannot reconcile it with the impossible horror of how they were severed from me in
an instant.

We talked about birthdays the day before the

wave, sitting in a jeep under a *weera* tree, while gab-
bling hornbills flitted about. Vik was to be eight
in a few months. Malli was annoyed that each year
Vik's birthday was before his. He asked us when *he*
would be eight. Steve explained that he had to be six
first, then seven, and only then eight. "Will Vik still
be eight when I am eight?" Steve confessed that Vik
would be ten then. Malli's outburst of "Aw, why do I
always have to be younger?" sent the hornbills scattering, and we too drove away.

Vik's eighth birthday arrived not even three
months after the wave. I was in the bedlam of my
mind. He is dead? For his birthday he'd wanted a
camera and a new cricket bag.

I recently opened Vik's cricket bag. I'd avoided
doing this for four and something years. I looked
at his bat and in every dent saw the flourish of his
hands striving for the perfect stroke. His red ball was
flecked with grass and mud. He nearly broke Steve's
middle finger once when bowling to him in our
garden—it wasn't his fault, Dad was stupid not to
wear gloves. In that bag were a helmet and kneepads
and sweat-soiled guards and yellowing white gloves.
And amid all that, a single leaf. A small dark brown
leaf with a pointed tip, I couldn't say what kind,
dried up and crisp but still intact, its threadlike
veins and jagged edges undamaged after all these
years. It crumbled a bit when I picked it up, dust on
my hands. Where did this come from? Our garden?

Or maybe Highgate Wood. Steve and Vik would play in the cricket nets there while I kept watch on Mal as he climbed a pyramid of logs and twigs or hid among the trees awhile before shouting out "Mum!" in a slight panic that I might have lost him.

Mum. Sometimes I find it hard to believe that I was their mum. Even as I remember fragments of their birth or recall how I reassured Malli as he peered from behind that tree, the truth that I was their mother is veiled in confusion. It is distant also. Was I really? Was it really me who could predict a looming earache from the color of their snot, who surfed the Internet with them looking for great white sharks, and who cuddled them in blue towels when they stepped out of the bath?

I know it was me, of course, but that knowing is cloudy and even startling at times. Strange. For one thing, they are dead, so what am I doing alive? I must be heartless. I am their mother. I am tortured, true, my dreams howl for them most nights, I am still as mutilated as I was in those first weeks when I couldn't step beyond the door because they weren't beside me. But this is hardly enough, surely my reactions nowhere near match the awfulness of their death. Yet nothing can, I suspect, fantasize as I might about hurling myself into that heaving ocean in Yala, doing it properly now, no clinging on to branches this time.

Is it because I am still dazed that I can't grasp the reality of being their mother? Is it because I am stunned by the way it ended that the truth of being their mother is muted? Maybe I willed it this way, in shock and desperation, when in an instant they were gone. I was so tightly wrapped around them, their moods and needs tugging at me always, but then I tried to unwind from them, determined and furious, insisting to myself that it was pointless keeping close to them, because I was no longer their mum. And even now, some four years on, I am hesitant to grab them with my heart, fierce and tender, the way I used to when they were alive. How can I bear to do that in this void? So I shy away from knowing Malli's weight in my arms as I carried him indoors when he'd fallen asleep in the car. I don't want to hear Vik ask me if he'd played well at his football class, in that uncertain tone he used when he knew he hadn't but needed me to reassure him with a lie. If I allow any of this, I will go mad for wanting them.

Won't I?

And maybe I forfeit being their mother because, at times, I feel helplessly responsible for their death. We took them back to Sri Lanka that December, Steve and I. Although we were only doing what we always did, and although it was those tectonic plates that slipped, I can't rid myself of the feeling that I led them to harm when they relied on me. So I am hesitant to evoke the intensity with which I watched over them. I can't tolerate knowing how they always counted on me. Yet occasionally, for a few moments, I cannot resist peeking into that life. When Google street maps went 3D in London recently, I looked at our street, and I was catapulted into being who I was with them. We walk to school, I tell them to zip up their jackets. Now they run ahead of me. "Don't tread on that dog shit, Vik," I hear myself say. If I didn't watch out, he always did that.

But I let my children go, when I was their mother. That jeep turned over in the surging water, and in all those minutes after, I have no idea how long, I didn't think of what became of them. There was that terrible crushing in my chest in the water, true, and I thought I was dying. But there was no shrieking refusal to leave, I didn't lament for them, for our life. *It's over, but what to do* was more precisely the thought that fluttered in my mind, and now I am startled by how wispy and casual this seems. I would have expected different. We were in our hotel room only moments before, it was Christmas the previous day, for crying out loud, and now in this ferocious water, all I could muster was a *what to do?* Although for some moments I wanted to stay alive for my boys, I soon gave up. Some mother.

When that jeep turned over, we dispersed. We

just slipped out, I guess, no moment of separation, not one that I was aware of anyway. It was not like I tried to cling to my children as they were torn from my arms, it was not like they were yanked from me, not like I saw them dead. They simply vanished from my life forever. In order to survive this bizarre and brutal truth, do I have to make murky the life I had with them?

That Malli wanted us to kiss his toe better whenever he stubbed it running barefoot in the garden. That a wave came for us when they were playing with their Christmas presents in a hotel room, when we weren't even in the ocean. Not knowing how to allow these two realities to coexist, I perhaps dim them both, intentionally or not, I don't know.

But I wasn't there when they most needed me. I know I was too powerless in that raging water to get to them, not that I knew where they were. Even so, I failed them. In those terrifying moments, my children were as helpless as I was, and I couldn't be there for them, and how they must have wanted me. Their helplessness I can't bear to consider, just as I turn away from the memory of Vik crying in fear as we sat for a few moments in that jeep before the water filled up. How can I hold the truth of being their mum when I have all this to live with?

There's more. I didn't even look for them. After the water disappeared. I let go of that branch, and I didn't search for my boys. I was in a stupor, true, I was shaking and shivering and coughing up blood. But still I berate myself for not scouring the earth for them. My screams should have had no end. Instead, I stared at the swampy scrub around me and told myself they were dead. I remember now. I even then wondered what I was going to do with my life. And in those weeks and months after, when my relatives and friends were combing the country for Malli, I took no notice, or I insisted it was pointless. Why did I so readily accept this hideous reality? Because I was desperate to protect myself from hope in case that hope became dust? Or because I truly knew? I cannot say. But I was their mother, and I should have reached for them in whatever way I could, however futile or impossible it seemed. I did not, I abandoned them, and that sickens me.

I might feel more like their mother if I was constantly weeping and screaming and tearing my hair out and clawing the earth, I think sometimes. Over these years I've only infrequently even come close to this. But why? My reactions are not natural, they are feeble, I feel, and I find this abhorrent. I am paralyzed without my family, true, but I expect something different. I remember being about eight years old and sitting cross-legged on the floor of our balcony at home in Colombo and swatting mosquitoes while listening to a woman from the shanty-town nearby wailing because her sister had died. For days and days, her shrieking and her swearing sliced the neighborhood with hardly a pause, and I was mesmerized, believing that's what you have to do when someone dies. That thought must still lurk in me, for every time I read about England winning a test match, or about Pluto no longer being a planet, I loathe myself for not howling endlessly, knowing Vik would be so rapt in all that. I might be less bewildered about being their mum, if I did. Then again, it's not like my mind isn't teetering when I read those words, it's not like I'm not wild inside.

I do have times of clarity, though, when I reunite with the truth of being their mother, quite unreservedly, without wincing or clenching. Sometimes vast isolated landscapes allow me this. Recently, my friend Malathi and I were in sub-Arctic Sweden, on the deserted shores of a lake of ice, surrounded by naked birches sheathed in frozen fog, each branch glowing like a stag's antlers in velvet in that mellow light. Immersed in that endless white, I knew I was their mother, my horror dormant, or not that relevant even. I burned with the knowledge of Malli's coziness on my lap. I allowed myself to know how his legs curled around me as he sat squeezing the hump of his toy camel, which blared out an Arabic pop song that irritated before long. And this was different from my usual hesitant, misty remembering. Perhaps that shimmering emptiness melted my defenses and untangled my mind and untwisted my heart. But I was startled by my boldness in trespassing so wholly back into that life.

It can also be like this when I am in our home in London, which is something I can't tolerate too much. On my last visit, I sat in the boys' bedroom wondering, was it really me who laid out their clothes on these beds each morning? I found Vik's favorite black sweatpants, faded to white at the knees. I touched them, and my confusion about putting out their clothes vanished. And lying on the floor, the pants clasped to my chest, I sobbed into them a good while, as a mother should. I only stopped when I looked in the pockets and found a wrapper from those Love Hearts sweets that boy was so greedy for. Steve would have given in and bought him that rubbish, not me. And I was as narked as I was then, remembering how Vik would suck on those sweets with glee, showing off what Daddy had got him, rolling the heart-shaped candy in his mouth, his tongue alight with that bright lemon, E-number-rich coloring. Disgusting.

Y ou were *spinning,*" she said. "Imagine that."

She'd been searching for a crocodile skull
when my friend Caryll met one of the men who
found me in that muddy jungle on the day of the
wave. The crocodile skull was for the museum.
Vikram and Malli's primary school in London, Holly
Park School, had a fund in their memory, and we
used the money to modernize the small wildlife
museum in Yala. It was on a bench there that I sat
in a daze in those first hours after the wave. Caryll
organized the renovations—she gets things done—
and that museum is now wonderfully transformed.

She related to me what this man, my rescuer,
told her. Until now I'd not been aware of this.

"He told me about finding you. It was definitely
he who found you. He gave the same story as you.
He said something very strange. It still gives me the
chills.

"The man is a park ranger. He said that on the
day of the tsunami, he was driving to the park with
some others when they heard something about a
tidal wave. They turned into the road to the hotel,
someone said the hotel has been hit. But the road
was flooded, they couldn't go on. They got out of
their van. It looked like the end of the world, he said.
No one knew what had happened. One of the men
with him started screaming, about demons destroy-

ing the world. Then they shouted, asking if anyone was alive, asking people to come out.

"A boy shouted for help. They went looking for him. Then they saw you. So it matches your story. He said you were wearing a dark blue top, sleeveless. That's what you were wearing, no? And he said you had no trousers on.

"But listen. He said you were the strangest sight he's ever seen. You were covered in black mud. No, listen, it gets weirder. He said you were spinning. Going round and round. Yes, spinning. Like children do when they want to get dizzy and fall. This man, I was talking to him in his office, and he rose from his chair and showed me what you doing. Spinning in that mud. He was so shocked, he said. You wouldn't stop.

"When he asked you to go with him, you refused. You wouldn't speak, but you kept shaking your head. He said you just went on spinning.

"One of the men wrapped his shirt around your waist. They dragged you quite a long way and put you in their van. They took you to the ticket office. Then they rushed off, they had to look for any others who might be alive. He said he has often wondered what happened to you.

"Also, listen. He described where he found you. It was not that far from the hotel, by the lagoon, actually. The water went all those miles inland. Then it turned and went back to the sea across the lagoon.

So you were carried all the way in and out again. You hung on to that tree just seconds before you would have been washed out to sea.

"That man, he keeps thinking about how you were spinning. Like you were in a trance. Maybe you were spinning in the water and couldn't stop? I asked him whether he was sure of this. Yes, yes, he kept saying. *Karaki karaki hitiya.* Imagine."

Six

On the Interstate 70 from Denver to Snowmass, Anita's daughter Kristiana asks me what a ghost town is. Her question startles me. For this is how it used to be. Me answering their questions, explaining things to her and Vik. About dung beetles and ant colonies, about capital cities and the rings around Saturn, about duck-billed dinosaurs. Sometimes I'd throw in a silly story to make them laugh. "When I was little, my friend in Sri Lanka ate the ants on her bottle of Orange Crush saying they were full of vitamin C. And they didn't bite her tongue." "Did she eat a whole ant colony?" "No, just half of one, I think." But now when Kristiana asks me about Colorado ghost towns, I offer only a stilted sentence. How can I answer her questions when Vik is not here? When Vik is not here to savor my replies or frown in distrust. How can I bring myself to tell her what I would have told them both? If Vik were here, they would have stories of the gold rush and prospectors, of exploding rocks and of railroads, of blasting tunnels in the mountains to find silver ore.

They were like siblings, Kristiana, her sister, and

my boys. The familiarity, the ease, the irritation, the fury, it was all there. Our families had been neighbors in London since Kristiana and Vikram were six months old. Alexandra and Malli didn't know a world without each other. And over the years, through combat and cooperation, the older two and the younger two became more and more alike, their interests and personalities calibrating to such an extent.

I can see us all on a Friday night. Anita, Agi, Steve, and I are in our kitchen. The table is scattered with bottles of red wine, the smell of the garlic and rosemary that Steve has stuffed into a leg of lamb escapes from the oven, and Abbey Lincoln's "When the Lights Go on Again" warms us. In the playroom, Vik is reading to Kristiana from *A Field Guide to the Birds of Sri Lanka* by G. M. Henry, his latest obsession. Sweet-natured as always, she tries to be eager about wingspans and the nesting habits of some obscure bird. The younger duo make regular trips to the toilet, taking turns to crouch and peer while the other does a wee. Their faces are thickly painted with crayons. An overturned sofa is a castle. And as the evening progresses, our conversations in the kitchen are interrupted by the sounds of our children's mayhem. But the wine is so good that not one of us wants to emerge from our mild stupor to investigate.

And now I am in a trance, traveling in the Colorado Rockies with Anita, Agi, and these girls who are so infused with my boys. Expressions, gestures, mannerisms, pronouncements all overwhelm me, coming at me fast, each a reflection of Vik and Mal. I want to avert my eyes, but I furtively seek them out, hungry for every one. Alexandra watches television, resting her chin on her fists in concentration. That's just how Malli would sit, and he would glower at me if I entered the room. *Leave me alone.* Now I see the four of them, rapt in an afternoon TV program, a blue bowl with tangerine pips balancing on the arm of our red sofa.

My mind fumbles. They should all be here. Vik and Malli should have gone skiing with the girls. The boys' faces should now be flushed from the sun and the wind and from jumping in and out of the hot tub. The four children would often bathe together in Anita's oversize bath, elbowing each other for a bit more space, soap bubbles popping on their cheeks. I can see it as if it's happening now. I want to lift Malli out of the tub and smell crayons on his face.

When the girls speak, my heart listens in fear of being blown apart by the knowledge of what would have been. When I project on my own what the boys would be doing now, my thoughts can be as nebulous as I want them to be. Not so with the girls' chatter, no fog to veil what they say.

One evening we talk a lot about Vik and Malli. We recall amusing incidents. The girls' faces shine as they speak of how Vik wanted a crow as a pet. I tell them about the three pet terrapins the boys had in Colombo. Malli named one of them Rover because what he really wanted was a dog. And when the terrapins got sick and died, I tell them, Steve and I worried that the boys would be sad, but Vikram fed the dead terrapins to the crows. Vik was so funny, says Alexi. And as her blue eyes flash in remembering, I am made acutely aware that so much of Vik and Malli still remains embedded in these girls. So how can I now want to escape from them? How can I shield my eyes and ears from them, even as they unwittingly send piercing bits of shrapnel my way? It all ended so impossibly for them, too. We went to Sri Lanka for Christmas, as usual, and never returned. Vikram is a good swimmer, he will swim through the wave, Kristiana kept saying in those bewildering early days. That was also when she began bouts of burping, loud and deliberate, something she never did before. It was our Vik who was the maestro of earsplitting burps. It's like she took on Vikram's spirit, Anita told me later. The more annoying bits of it, at least.

Kristiana has a stomachache and is asleep on my lap. Vikram would sleep on me like this, the weight sinking into me, the intermittent wriggling to get comfortable. This could be Vik. A strand of hair falls across her face, and I push it back. Her hair is not drenched in sweat. Vik always sweated when he slept on my lap. And now as I sit here and look out at the snow peaks of the Rockies glowing in the lowering sun, the refrain *Vikram will never sleep on my lap* cinders me. Kristiana stirs, clutches her stomach, and whimpers a little. I run my fingers through her hair to keep her asleep until the Calpol makes her tummy ache better, exactly as I would do with Vikram.

LONDON, 2009

The blackout blinds in the boys' bedroom never really did their job. They wouldn't pull all the way down, so in the summer the light came in way too early. A strip of sun stole across the carpet and lit up an open book or made one of yesterday's green socks glow. That was all it took to stir Vik. In an instant he'd be at the window, telling his brother to wake up quick, the foxes might be in the garden. I'd give up trying to sleep through their shouts of "Fox! Fox!" and stagger downstairs to free them into the glorious morning. Those faulty blinds meant hours of fun before school. Five summers ago, that was, yet it seems like no time at all.

Each time I return to our home, I am nervous. Maybe it's best to go another time, I tell myself. How can I even glimpse the intolerably fresh green outside?

The garden bulges with early summer, now as it did then. Late-evening shadows darken the grass. Rosebushes flicker in the smattering of last light that leaks through next door's willow. Two plump robins drift across the lawn to swing on the honeysuckle, so tame they almost flick my arm. I spot a purple manta ray. Malli would skip along this flowerbed with armfuls of plastic ocean life. Steve and Vik would sit under the apple trees and eat sardines on toast. Five summers without them in this garden.

But it's different, my visit to our home this time. When I returned previously, I could endure only cautious glances at my family. I looked now and again but mostly wanted to keep them a blur. Now I can hardly take my eyes off them, quite unlike when they were alive. So I investigate, constantly. I am rediscovering them, almost. I amass details of them, and us.

These five years I've been so fearful of details. The more I remember, the more inconsolable I will be, I've told myself. But now increasingly I don't tussle with my memories. I want to remember. I want to know. Perhaps I can better tolerate being inconsolable now. Perhaps I suspect that remembering won't make me any more inconsolable. Or less.

This house sparks and almost still chimes with them.

On a counter in the kitchen there are a couple of CDs, out of their covers. In those last months, Steve played these for the boys, music from his youth. Vik would jump up and down gracelessly to "Our House" by Madness. The three of them would belt out Ian Dury's "Hit Me with Your Rhythm Stick"— yelling the words "'It's nice to be a lunatic, hit me!'" That energy, I can retrieve it now. It still crackles within these walls.

An old shoebox lets out the smell of Sunday evenings. It's Steve's shoe-polishing box. I rummage in it. Together with the polishes and the brushes, there is the rag he used for that final buff, the same one he'd had for years and years. He'd sit on the stairs on a Sunday evening and shine his shoes and the boys'. I hold that rag to my nose, and it still smells of the start to our week. My face is wet with crying. Yet how welcome, this old rag that tells me it was true, our life.

This is my worst day of life. These words are written in Vik's handwriting on the sofa in the playroom. I'm taken aback. I've never seen this. Not before the wave or after. Why did he write it? Something I did? A playground fight that upset him and I ignored? Then I see some football scores he's written on the arm of the sofa—Liverpool lost. For some moments I'm relieved. But then, how much I want to console him, and I am helpless.

In these past years, I've pushed away thoughts of my children's everyday hurts and fears, suggestions of their frailty and tenderness. It's easier to remember my boys with humor or to recall their cheek. But now as I dare to peer more closely at them, they emerge more whole.

For years I've told myself it's pointless to cherish my children's personalities and their passions, for they are now dead. But here in our home I am surrounded by proof of it all. I unlock my mind a little and allow myself to know the wonder of them.

Our friends often remarked that our boys were remarkably focused on what enthused them, almost unusually so for their ages. I sometimes wished Malli could be distracted from his theatrics, so he might learn to spell. Everything in our living room—a brocade throw, a carved wooden window frame from Nepal, a brass cobra—was a prop for the "shows" he plotted and fervently rehearsed. That fantasy world he moved in. With his collection of puppets and his swirl of costumes, he was constantly morphing a new story into being. His imaginings were often curious. In our study I find a typically toddler painting of blue and brown blotches. Malli did this when he was about three. "Nice, nice, Mal. What is it?" I asked him then, distractedly. "A man who lost his hands in a puddle," he replied, not stopping to think.

Steve and I encouraged our son's meanderings, defending him when his teacher complained that he held up the science lesson by insisting that cars were alive. But I worried about Malli's five-year-old cunning the day he deliberately tripped his brother up on the street. I wasn't there, our nanny described what happened, and Vik had a gash on his head. "And the police saw you doing this and called me to complain," I scolded, taking my own story too far now. He believed me but was undaunted. "They didn't say what time it happened, did they? They didn't say what color the two boys were, maybe the boys were white, some other boys." "Will he be a criminal or a judge?" I later asked Steve.

Their promise, my children's possibilities, still linger in our home.

Everywhere in this house are sheets of A4 filled with Vik's calculations, all sorts. Vik was quite astonishingly quick. I sit on our bed and remember those hours before bedtime when he would be beside me, intent on some math problem he'd pestered me for. The boy grasped concepts effortlessly, and Steve and I had to keep him curious. He'd recite to us minutiae about some aspect of the natural world he was fanatical about. He inhaled information about whatever creature stirred him, and often it seemed he became one with them. When he was younger, he'd stand in front of the brachiosaurus skeleton in the Natural History Museum in London (that place was our second home, Vik could walk through it blindfolded), his neck stretching out, his body contorting, as he fused with the giant sauropod. More recently, I'd noticed how he watched eagles, easing into their glide, the raptor's eyes in his.

Vik and I would lie together on his bed and chat, in that calm half-hour before his bedtime. His eyes would be afire as he told me about the theater group that had visited his school that day, everyone in his class took part in *The Tempest*, it was brilliant, he was Prospero. Or I'd flick through his cricket magazine and say, "Wow, he's handsome," at a photo of

Rahul Dravid. "Aw, who do you love, Mum, Dad or Dravid?" he'd admonish me, quick to look out for Steve, the king of dads. Now I sit alone on the same bed, and our easy companionship, Vik's and mine, returns with such exactness. I can see him, rolling up his pajamas to carefully peel away a scab on his knee. And I don't insist myself back to reality as I usually do. Maybe it is not so overwhelming after all, to dissolve the divide between now and then.

But this does make me mad with wanting them. I let myself miss them more unreservedly now, at times at least. I rein in my yearning less. So I lie under the apple trees at the foot of our garden, on a mat still flecked with our picnics, and look up at two empty bird feeders that Steve once tied to the branches. And I want more than anything to hear my boys natter on a Saturday morning as they fill those feeders with "birdie nuts."

Maybe yearning for them more freely gives me some relief. When I tried to tame my ache for them, especially here in this house, it didn't ease my pain. On my earlier visits here, in the evenings especially, their absence came bounding at me off walls and trees, the desolation clobbered me. There is a difference now. Their absence is not so heavy, not so leaden, it seems. I sleep wearing Steve's sarong, and I remember trying to inch away from him as he insisted on sleeping wrapped up in me. And how badly I still want that. Yet I am warmed by this knowing and this wanting. It helps me to better tolerate the bareness of our bed.

By knowing them again, by gathering threads of our life, I am much less fractured. I am also less confused. I don't constantly ask, *Was I their mother?* How can so much of my life not even seem like mine?

I can recover myself better when I dare let in their light.

There are red pen marks rising up a wall in our living room where Steve and I would measure the boys' heights. I see those inexact squiggles and instantly lean right back into who I was. I know it was me who settled those squabbles about who had grown the most. I know it was me who scolded Malli for standing on tiptoe to be taller, his heels right up on those slightly peeling skirting boards on that wall. And yes, it was me who'd tell Vik that it was silly to drink half a pint of milk just before I measured him—you won't get instantly taller, now will you? And without thinking I lightly kiss those red Biro marks just as I would the tops of their heads. Then I slump to the floor with my back against that wall.

*H*ere in our home of all places, I am surprised to find that, sometimes at least, they leave me alone. In the green dusk of our garden, a daddy longlegs stumbles along the rim of my chilled wineglass. Then I remember. It was at this time of year that we moved into this house.

It was one of those rare hot June days in London, much like today. I'd always coveted these strapping Edwardian houses, their redbrick exteriors radiant in the sun. And we'd found one just right for us, easy, inviting, not likely to be ruffled by our chaos. For now we could live with its imperfections, such as the swirling green and mustard carpet in the hallway that looked like it belonged in a pub in the 1970s. We'll pull it up soon and repair those cracked original tiles underneath, of course, but no rush.

And I can see our first evening here, Steve spread out on the lawn after the removal men had left, hands locked under his head, sun and relief and a smile on his face. Vik and Malli, then four and nearly two, hiding in packing boxes indoors, a little lost because they could no longer shout over the fence to their friends next door. And Malee, our nanny, insisting on cooking *kiribath* and boiling milk in a new clay pot until it spilled over, for plenty and good luck. For even more good fortune, Steve insisted on playing the *pirith* tape my mother had sent from Colombo. He'd kept it on repeat all day, and I turned the volume down so the removal men wouldn't be distracted by chanting Buddhist monks.

We had lived in this house three and something years when we left for Colombo that night in early December. And we still hadn't got rid of that hall carpet. But we had plans for the next summer, to redecorate the whole house, move the boys into separate bedrooms. By converting the loft, Steve and I could finally have our own studies.

With each visit back to the house in this last year, I grew more and more impatient with the ugly hall carpet. Yet how could I throw it out? The boys would sit on it to put on their shoes every morning, that's where they'd fling their jackets down when they came in from school. Still, despite my hesitations, that carpet is now gone. I rebuked myself once I was rid of it. How could I have tossed their footprints out? Yet I keep admiring my new floor, the hallway is so much brighter now. But why does it matter, why do I care? They are not here. So what am I doing? Playing house?

Malli often did that, with his friend Alexandra. Played house. And that's exactly what she did the first time she came back to our home after the wave. She walked straight into our playroom, pulled out the dolls' house from a corner, and played house, as if she'd been here just yesterday. She remembered it, she said, although she was last in that room more than four years ago, and then she was not yet five.

In those months and months after the wave, I could hardly bear to hear the names of my children's friends. And when I began to see them again, I was afraid of being reminded of how my boys would be, of knowing what they are missing. I see my children's friends often now. They are bubbling over when we meet, I enjoy their sparkle. And they make my boys real, so they are not beyond my field of vision, as they were in those first years.

Kristiana and Alexandra are over whenever I am back in the house. They help me water the garden, we discuss their homework, they punch the doors wearing Vik's boxing gloves. They drum on Malli's tabla. And I remember him twirling frenetically but with quite remarkable rhythm to the soundtrack from *Lagaan,* delicious in his Jaipuri turban, with its long tail wafting behind him, the quickening pulse at the end of "Chale Chalo" making him utterly dizzy.

But I am an empty-handed mother. I can't offer Vik to these girls to make them laugh at his silly jokes. I can't give them Malli, so he and Alexi can talk about getting married—or "merried," as Malli would say—as they often did. "You are mad to get married, Mal," Vik would say to his brother. "Your wife will boss you around, she will shout at you from the upstairs window when you're coming home from work." Where that boy got his ideas about marriage from, I don't know.

Now Alexi is in our living room wearing the same red school uniform that my boys wore. A long thread dangles from the frayed cuff of her sweatshirt, the boys' sweaters were always worn around the cuffs like this. I look at Alexi, and for a moment I wonder, really, am I in this life or that?

She snaps me out of it, this nine-year-old girl. "*Why* did they have to die?" she asks suddenly and loudly, with great drama, throwing herself on a pile of cushions. "How can *five* of them die?" I have no words. "Was it scary when the wave came?" she goes on, never mind my discomfort. I tell her it happened fast. She ponders this for a while before saying, "If you and Steve had died and Vikram and Malli had survived, will they have come to live with us?" As she waits expectantly for my answer, I realize that this is her preferred scenario, and it's something she's been wondering about for years. I say, "Yes, of course." She smiles. "Oh *good*. So my mum has your house keys, right? So we would have come and got their things and brought them to our house, right?" For days later I carry that image, a forlorn Vik and Malli standing outside our front door, having come "to get their things."

Five years, and how my children's friends have

grown. My boys would have too. I am increasingly
curious now when I see their friends. My eyes can't
stop probing, so I can better picture Vik and Mal.
I meet Vikram's mates Daniel and Joe for the first
time in five years. Joe towers above me as he hugs
me so gently. He is nearly thirteen. A fist flies out
of nowhere and knocks me down hard. This is how
Vik would look. I am transfixed by the changes in
these two boys. I stare into what I will never know
in my own life, a speck of acne, broadening shoulders, a hint of facial hair. It is strangely satisfying,
projecting my boys into the present like this. But
Vik enjoyed the company of his mates so much. And
here am I with them, when he can't be. I feel I am
handling contraband.

Our life is also kindled when I go back to our
old haunts. I avoided these places until recently, and
I insisted I'd never return. But slowly I am finding
the nerve to revisit them. Sarah and I go walking
on the borders of Hampstead Heath, one of Steve's
favorite places in London to roam. The four of us
were here just some days before we left for Colombo
that December. And I have not been back until now.
The hedges along the paths are quick with finches,
and it's as though I've never been away. It's hard to
believe that we were not together here last Saturday.
I know each tree we would picnic under, I know
where the boys tried to play rugby with their dad. I

see the spot where Steve led them to tackle me to the ground as I foolishly ambled over to throw back the ball they'd lobbed at me. The ground was all muddy, I was wearing white jeans, and they were wildly hysterical. Amused I was not.

*M*alli was about two when he began telling us about his real family. We were his family, too, but he had another family, his "real family." "I am going back to them," he'd say. "I am staying with you only a little time."

"So what's your real dad's name?" Steve would ask. "Tees." "*Tees*? What kind of weird name is that?" "Don't laugh, Dad, it's a *real* name." "And your mum?" "Sue. And I have a sister. Her name is Nelly."

He said he loved his sister the most. They lived in America. "Our house is near a big lake, we have a boat even, we *do*. It's in Merica."

Malli was undeterred by Vikram's smirks and the incredulity of his little friends. "But you don't have a sister, Mal. Where is she? Show me." "Don't be silly, Alexandra, she can't come here. She's in another country, Merica."

My mother and our nanny, Malee, insisted that he was talking about a past life. "This is just the age some children remember their previous birth," they'd say. They sometimes asked that Steve and I "do something" about it, go to the temple, talk to a priest.

All we did was entertain our children by pretending to be Malli's "real" parents, we'd do it for whole weekends sometimes. Steve proposed they lived in rural Mississippi. The boys had raucous fun when

he acted as Tees coming to London to visit Malli.
In his rather comic version of a southern accent, he
would launch into tirades about how crowded the
big city was and how he missed the mosquitoes of
the swamps. "Again, again, Dad. Do Tees again!"

Malli ended the story of his real family some
months before the wave. "Mal, where are Sue and
Tees now? Are they still in America?" Vik asked him
one day, teasingly. "They're dead," came the reply.
"They went to Africa and were eaten by lions." "All
of them? Lions don't usually eat so many people at
once," said Vik, ever the naturalist. "Yes, all of them.
I just got the message." "Message from whom, Mal?"
He didn't reply.

Seven

*E*ven the lizards have left, it seems. Those small green and brown creatures with their ancient heads and sticklike tails would be forever scuffling in this grass, alert to Vik stalking them with his fishing net. But nothing stirs in this wilted garden today. Nearly six years after the wave, and five years of other people living in it, my parents' home is transformed. Empty now, it cringes with neglect. Leaves from the jak tree litter the back veranda. My mother never liked that jak tree. It towers in the middle of the garden, and she thought it far too big. She fretted that it would come crashing down in a strong wind one day and destroy the house.

I was seven when we moved to this house. On our first night here my parents had a *pirith* ceremony to bless our new home. For hours the monks hummed, and I sat distracted by the rows of little clay lamps that flickered around our pond. For me then, that pond was the most marvelous thing about our new home. It was indoors and had no roof over it. I was curious, how will it be when the rains come? This house changed over the years because changing the house was one of my mother's passions. Dining rooms were enlarged, all glass and open to the garden, terrazzo floors were dug out and replaced with marble. And the pond disappeared. It was paved over because it overflowed during the monsoons, and Ma got tired of goldfish gasping on her new floors.

I've not stepped into this house since those early months after the wave, when I wandered through it, stunned. I've come back now eager for details of us, of my parents especially. I want to make our life in Sri Lanka real, less of a dream.

But this is quite unlike being in our home in London, where it feels as though we've just stepped out. There our life is affirmed, whereas in this strangeness it falters. Did my father really read his newspaper on this veranda, on that ebony armchair with the armrest that kept falling off? Did my boys wake in this bedroom at night disturbed by polecats pelting on the ceiling, and did I really hush them into sleep, my fingers combing their hair?

I turn on a light in the living room, even though it is daytime. The familiar feel of that confusing jumble of switches on the wall, and I perk up. I wash my hands in a bathroom upstairs and feel a lightness from the touch of the tap. Sunlight streams into that bathroom, and I sit on the toilet and let it scorch my back. The relief of habit. I don't hear the tinkle of my mother's gold bangles ("Aachchi's bells," Vik called that sound), but these walls have knowledge of it. My life coheres a little.

It is July. We'd be here every July for the summer holidays. The house gusted with my children's chaos. My parents filled our days with big ceremonial meals. Pork curry blackened with roasted coconut on Monday, hoppers on Tuesday, biryani on Wednesday, and god forbid if Steve and I planned to go out to dinner with friends on other days. Ma would be glum and announce that someone she knows ate at the restaurant we were going to and had diarrhea, for a whole week would you believe. For my mother, no one could cook as well as she and her three sisters, and she wasn't far wrong. During English winters, Steve craved her prawn curry, her signature dish. The fiery-red gravy was thickened with a paste made by grinding the half-cooked heads of the prawns, something she'd learned from her grandmother.

It's four o'clock in the afternoon, and there are three triangles of sunlight trembling on the floor of this veranda, now as there were then. I can almost hear them out here. My mother and my aunts.

Together they were wayward, Ma and her three sisters. Mostly they laughed. Their laughter was a constant in my life, and in this house. As a child I was perturbed by just how much they laughed. I thought it unbecoming, other mothers and aunts didn't get so hysterical surely? But always I felt safe within their merriment.

I could never resist being regaled by the stories that set them off. There was endless gossip. Someone emptied a flower vase, water and all, on the head of her husband's mistress at the hairdresser's. And stories from when they were young girls—my grandfather, a serious-minded civil servant, lined his four daughters up at the men's barber's and ordered severe short haircuts so they'd be unattractive and no boy would take a second look. Then there were descriptions of my grandparents' later attempts to arrange suitable marriages for them. Michael, their squint-eyed gardener, would be the first to glimpse and pronounce on these proposed suitors. *"Eeya, haamu, eeya"* (Yikes, madam, yikes), he'd whisper through the window to Ma and her sisters as a hapless, oily-haired man stepped out of a Morris Minor.

And they laughed at us, when we were children. They thought it hilarious when I was distraught that time we holidayed in a dirty bungalow in Elephant Pass in the north of Sri Lanka. I was fourteen and wanted to be partying in Colombo, not stuck out in this remoteness with only an enormous lagoon and a train that went past once every night. "Come watch the train," they'd say to me, chuckling, and I'd sob. I remember the mirth my cousin Krishan caused when he was a little boy learning to read—he struggled with the word *right.* " 'Every cat has a *rigit* to eat fish,'" he would read with aplomb, a cat food advertisement on the back of a *Reader's Digest*. His mother and aunts would shriek with glee and press two rupees into his hand.

On an afternoon like today, Ma and my aunt Swyrie would be sitting out on this veranda, trying to outdo each other in not eating the chocolate cake on the table beside them because it would make them fat. Not looking fat mattered. I scolded them when they took it too far with that man selling bee's honey in the Habarana jungles—on another vacation that was. This almost toothless man, with straggly long hair and clad only in a loincloth, spent his days collecting wild honey, holding a flare to the mouths of beehives high up on trees and smoking out the bees. He was sitting in a forest glade when we met him, squeezing out liquid from the honeycomb with both hands, his long fingernails stained and gnarled. Pleased with the prospect of a quick sale, he held forth on the medicinal properties of his honey. Ah, but is it fattening? asked my mother or aunt. He looked at the two of them, alien species with lipstick and large sunglasses, and unsure of the correct response replied in his singsong voice, "Those who are too fat lose weight, those who are thin gain." "So what do you think will happen to us then?" they pestered him, giggling. Mortified by their ridiculous vanity, I quickly made them pay him and leave.

Now, in this house, I can bring my parents close.

For six years I've pushed them and their death to the fringes of my heart. That's all I could tolerate, my focus was on our boys and Steve. How hideous, that there should be a pecking order in my grief.

Often, in the far corner of this veranda, by the garden, there would be a seamstress bent over an ancient Singer sewing machine, *tuk-a-tuk-a-tuk-a,* I can hear her now. There was invariably something Ma urgently needed sewn. My mother was always elegant and paid careful attention to how she dressed. Except for the day before my wedding, when she was so busy and distracted that she rushed downstairs in the morning wearing a silk blouse and her usual sequined sandals but no trousers.

A few days before we left for Yala, Ma's seamstress made some dressing-up clothes for Malli. A parrot outfit and a large blue satin sack adorned with gold stars for his costume collection: his Christmas presents. He wore his parrot outfit on Christmas night, and it was tight around the ankles. We'll have it altered when we get back to Colombo tomorrow, Ma told Malli. Now I remember: some months after the wave, when I was scouring the ruins in Yala, I found that blue sack. It was entangled on the branch of a dead tree, intact, the satin still agleam.

I sit on the floor of my parents' bedroom, and it seems vast now, cleared of its furniture. Ma would

drape her saris standing in front of the mirror
that hung on one wall. I can see her fasten a pleat,
reaching for a pin from a white porcelain bowl, the
pin beaded with a tiny button so the silk wouldn't
tear. Her saris were her art, they filled mothballed
wardrobes in their bedroom and in her dressing
room. She despaired that I didn't show adequate
enthusiasm for her collection. "Who's going to wear
all these saris when I am dead? I don't know why I
bother to buy so many," she'd say. Or she'd tell me,
"You are so boring, such a shame you became an
academic. I saw some women like you going to a
conference the other day, so badly dressed, I wanted
to cry." Malli was her hope, he understood glamour
and flair. "Tell your mum to wear prettier clothes,
more makeup," she'd say to him as he stretched out
on her bed admiring his collection of small scented
soaps. On our last night in this house, I did dress
up, and both my mother and son approved. It was
the evening of Malli's violin concert, and I wore one
of Ma's saris, a crimson silk. Malli watched me dab
on some lipstick and told me he had his own lipstick, I could use it if I liked. Next time, I said.

My parents' bedroom leads to the balcony on
which my mother enacted her daily farce with the
fishmonger. Each morning he'd arrive at the gates
screaming out the contents of the baskets tied to
the pole he had slung across his shoulders. She'd
yell to him that she needed nothing, although she

intended to buy his entire catch, and he'd leave, loudly disgruntled, full well knowing he'd be back. They'd repeat this for some hours before he emptied his baskets by the gate, his day's work quickly done, and Ma would have more fish than she needed but at half his asking price. Steve would look at the crows and flies rushing to the bloodstained gravel by the gate and ask my mother if there was not a more efficient way to shop.

My parents helped Steve and me negotiate life in Colombo. In their minds we were still children, needing to be looked after. And in these years I've not permitted myself to yearn for their care. I'd feel even more perilously alone if I did, I've thought. Yet here in our home, snug in these familiar surroundings, I can't help but crave their comfort. Each night my father would stand on this balcony smoking his last cigar for the day. I want the smell of that smoke to reach me now and make my eyes sting just as it did then, although then I always complained about it.

I settle into our life in this house and am suddenly chilled. As always, I think about how I didn't stop. When we ran from those waves, I didn't stop at the door of my parents' hotel room. I decided not to. A split second it was, and I didn't know then what we were running from or running to, but I decided that.

The last time I saw my mother, it was the night before the wave. After dinner on the terrace of the hotel, I said goodnight to her. I was hurried, the boys were tired, and I was taking them to bed. Goodnight was all I said. My father I saw the next morning when he knocked on our door to take back the pair of binoculars that Vik had borrowed from him. He was packing to leave. I only half-opened my eyes. Why are you packing so early, why do you have to be so bloody organized, I thought.

He always was meticulous. His study is vacant now. I drift in this space that once had such order. Over there by the door was where his black lawyer's robes used to hang. I twirl my fingers in the dust on the bare bookshelves that line the walls.

For some thirty years I spent time with my father in this room, browsing his library. When I was about ten, I discovered the tranquillity of my father's study at night and began to explore his vast book collection. I would sit cross-legged on the floor here, immersed in *The Jungle Tide* by John Still. I learned that you could understand an elephant's mood from its footprints, that you could tell if it was running in fear or ambling in hope of water. I was transfixed by the tales of jungle gods—anyone who didn't make them an offering of two leaves fixed on a twig, they'd smite with blindness. My wonder and enthusiasm pleased my father. He was a reserved and contained man, and it was among his books that we began to savor each other's company.

In these past six years I've recoiled from remem-

bering my childhood. I felt foolish about my youth-
ful contentment, was niggled by a notion that even
as an unsuspecting child I must have been marked,
doomed. But now here in the home I lived in as a
child, I am more open to glimpses of what a glo-
riously happy time it was. Apart from when our
dachshund Nutmeg was severed in two by a double-
decker bus.

I remember being mindlessly happy when as a
teenager I made my brother late for school by adjust-
ing and readjusting myself at the mirror by the
front door when he was waiting for me in the car,
our driver anxiously sounding the horn. I remember
being a contented eight- or nine-year-old listening
to our old ayah Seelawathie tell us stories of *yakkas*
(demons) on nights my parents were out. Sometimes
I'd fuss before they'd leave—why do you have to go
dancing again?—and they'd calm me with a spoon-
ful of cough syrup and rush out, my mother wearing a puffed-up hairpiece and a glitzy nylon sari, so
fashionable in Colombo in the 1970s. Dozy with the
medicine, I'd join Seelawathie in reciting the names
of a long list of *yakkas* whom she insisted were
nearby, hovering around us. Demons didn't matter
to me, I felt safe in this house.

Years later when I was at Cambridge, every summer I brought friends back to my home. They had
never been to Asia before, and these English boys
would be impressed by the din of crickets as they sat

out on the lawn at night drinking whiskey with my father. My mother patiently took David to the doctor about his dodgy stomach while he expounded to her the urgency of world revolution, sitting in the back of her chauffeur-driven car. And one summer I shamelessly two-timed Steve and another boyfriend, Sri Lankan, not stopping for a moment to imagine that one day Steve and I would be creating a home for our sons in this house.

You have two homes, Steve and I always told the boys, and "Aachchi house" is your Colombo home. They needed to be rooted here, growing up as English–Sri Lankan children in London. And they went from one home to another, and from one country to another, effortlessly.

In this house my parents thrived as grandparents. They spoiled my children and took on their interests and curiosities with vigor and delight. I was amused by how my mother would willingly "go in goal" in the back garden while Vikram slammed a football at her. Vik would sit on my father's lap in his study and read books about man-eating tigers in India. Ma was as wound up as Vik in the days before another Harry Potter book came out. Malli never understood the need to wait for a sequel. "Why can't you get a pirate copy?" he'd ask, paying little heed when his grandfather told him in his lawyerly way that you couldn't pirate books that were unwritten and that it was, in fact, wrong to pirate anything.

"When I grow up I'm going to be *sooo* smart," Malli would say. "I'm going to make pirate DVDs and make pirate books before anyone writes them."

I invite monks to the house to perform a Buddhist ceremony, one that passes on merit to the dead. My parents observed these rituals. Now in their living room that is fragrant with freshly cut jasmines and incense, three monks sit on chairs that have been draped with pristine white cloth. One of the monks strikes a match and lights the brass oil lamp on the table in front of him. He unwinds a reel of white thread and passes it among me and my friends, who are sitting across from the monks on woven grass mats spread on the floor. Then the three monks begin their invocations. But as they harmonize their chanting, I still find it inconceivable that my family left this house one December morning and never came back. If anything, tonight feels like my very first night in this house, some thirty-five years ago, when there were more monks and more chants and life here was about to begin. I hold on to the white thread that's being blessed with prayer and conjure those other glowing oil lamps around the now-absent pond.

*D*o I dare open it? It's Steve's work diary for 2004. Two thousand four, our last year. The diary is in a bag of our things in my aunt's house in Colombo. In these past years I've picked it up, then hidden it away, panicked. Steve always wrote more than work appointments in his diaries. They were filled with reminders to take the children for haircuts, our plans for weekends and holidays, and notes to himself like (after he and I had a quarrel) "Tell S she was right, make up."

For most of that last year, until September, we lived in Sri Lanka. It was a blissful time. Steve and I had been wanting this for a while, an extended stay instead of the usual rushed holiday. So when we both had sabbaticals, we went to Colombo. We took the boys out of school in London and enrolled them in one there. I've kept that time distant in my mind these past six years. I especially didn't want to consider our unsuspecting joy and ease.

I am now in Colombo for the summer with Steve's sister Beverley, her husband, Chris, and their children, Sophie and Jack. Steve's family has made regular trips to Sri Lanka in the time since the wave, sometimes twice yearly. My niece and nephew are almost as intimate with life here as my boys were. In those early days I convinced myself that Steve's family must blame me for bringing him here, getting him killed. But then my father-in-law came to Colombo and held my hand and told me that Steve was always so happy here, that for him it was also home.

Encouraged by my in-laws, I opened Steve's diary. It was all there. Details of our nine months in Sri Lanka. I didn't read much, I quickly hid the diary away. But since looking into it I can't escape the memories of that last year. I reenter that time constantly. Strange, though, how for six years these thoughts have held back.

The beggar at the traffic lights on Horton Place has no arms. My niece Sophie reaches into her bag to give him some money. I've seen him so often in these last years, but only now do I remember. This beggar would be at these same traffic lights when we drove the boys to and from school that year. Steve gave him a weekly "allowance" to stop him weaving through traffic to get to our car each day, but it didn't work. My mother's driver insisted that Steve was being unnecessarily charitable. He claimed this man had blown up his own arms while trying to make a bomb to kill a neighbor, a rumor most likely. Our children also disapproved of this armless man. "Why can't he do a *job*?" Vik would say, alarming Steve and me by his lack of compassion.

I remember now, the boys were often grouchy on the way to school. This Colombo school was boring, they wished they were with their friends in London, the playground here was small. My declaring that they were having a wonderful new experience did nothing. Steve used music to improve their mood. He'd play the Susheela Raman track "Love Trap" in the car. When they heard the lyrics "'Your body is a love trap . . . Your honey lips are impossible to resist,'" the boys would liven up in disgust. "Ugh. Body. Lips, *yuk*." "Are you sure?" I'd say to Steve about his child-cheering-up tactics. But Vik and Malli stepped out of the car deliriously grossed out and ready for school.

We had rented a house in central Colombo during that time. Whenever I've passed that street in these years since the wave, I've looked the other way or pretended to myself it was of no significance. Now I drive down this narrow lane with my in-laws. And I can see them, Steve and Malli, walking up here. Malli has his doll in a stroller, they are playing "Dads and Dads."

Time snaps back. It was just this morning we were all here, surely. Vik grew big and strong that year, I can feel now how the muscles on his thighs were hardening. He was seven, but I was buying clothes for a twelve-year-old. In Colombo, he was always playing sports, exciting Steve with his skill at cricket, keeping pace with his dad when every evening they sliced across the large swimming pool in my old school. I'd tell them to get lost when they played football on blazing afternoons and came back wet and shirtless with arms stretched out for a hug. I can't bear to walk into those playing fields, where I feel their footprints must still be fresh.

I've berated myself continually for bringing my family back to Sri Lanka that December. What was the need? We had only recently returned to London. We did too much, rushing between two countries, wanting it all, we couldn't get enough. I had it all, and I blew it, I've thought. In the early weeks after the wave, I'd have recurring dreams of my very mild-tempered friend Fionnuala striding down our street in London, screaming at me furiously for taking my children back to Colombo that Christmas.

But this summer, as I am more alive to those months we spent here, I accuse myself less. I can see why Steve and I decided to return. We wanted some continuity with the life we'd established.

That year, away from our usual routine in London, we had time. Steve and I worked on our research projects and papers. On holidays and week-ends the four of us traveled.

We hiked in the rain forest, often. We'd wake in the dark for the dawn chorus. I haven't heard that divine song in some six years, I can't bear to, but I re-member it vividly now. The distant bubbling erupted into cooing and pealing interspersed with the panic of parakeets and the *kruk-krukking* of jungle fowl. And above all that, the fluting of a spot-winged thrush, and higher still, the clarion whistle of a warbler.

We were frequently on the beach. Vik and I

would walk on the empty morning sand to watch arrack-breathed fishermen draw in their nets as the crows went wild. Steve made sashimi with the freshest tuna that was just off the boat, he relished that, proclaiming it "the dog's bollocks." Now I have a memory of us on a beach, eating gunnysack loads of mussels, steamed only in their own juices on an open fire. The clatter of slurped-out shells on a tin plate, salt on the children's eyelashes, sunset. Malli called this time of day "the sky is upon the table time." That was his version of the early lines of T. S. Eliot's "Prufrock." I don't know quite why, I often recited them to the boys.

We went to Yala many times. We'd been taking the boys there even before they could walk. We explored the scrub in a jeep, the heat rising off cratered tracks, our hair matted with powdery red dust. Vik understood the jungle, and I loved that. He'd be the first to spot a stone plover on a showery beach, he knew the long lush whistle of a bush lark. We always stayed at the same hotel. Each time we were there, Vik bought a "Checklist of Yala Birds" from the souvenir shop. I found these booklets in that same bag where Steve's 2004 diary was. Vik had marked off in them the birds he'd seen on each trip. I flicked through quickly, on each page his happy little ticks in a red pen.

I've been returning to Yala over these years, and on the drive from Colombo when I've approached the Udawalawe reservoir, I've always looked away. Vikram loved this spot, where hawks sail upwind above the gleaming water. On the night of the twenty-sixth of December 2004, when I was being driven back to Colombo, I hid my head between my knees as that van raced along the reservoir. I can't look because Vik will never see this again, I thought then. Six years later, I am on this same road with Steve's sister and her family. But for the first time since the wave, when we come to the reservoir, I am able to look.

Our nine-month stay in Sri Lanka in 2004 ended on the first of September. We were back in our garden in London just as the apples were turning red. In school, the boys got badges at morning assembly for settling back well. So when Steve and I discussed plans for the Christmas holidays, it wasn't hard to decide. The boys had rooted themselves well in Colombo, we should keep that connection close. Even a short trip would be fine. Just three weeks.

As always, Steve wrote in his diary various tasks he had to do in those three weeks. A deadline for a paper, a conference call, chores. I saw he'd written the date and time of our flight from London to Colombo, nine p.m. on December 8. There was no note about our flight back on the thirty-first, maybe he meant to do that later. But scrawled across the twenty-fourth, twenty-fifth, and twenty-sixth was the last word he wrote in that diary for 2004. *Yala.*

*T*hey never left. The wave didn't scare away the pair of white-bellied sea eagles that nested by the lagoon near the Yala hotel. When I first came back here after the wave and spotted them, I didn't dare watch. These were Vik's eagles, not mine. Then I became compulsive. I needed to see them each time I returned. I couldn't leave until I had at least a glimpse. I wanted their reassurance. But, please, I asked myself, reassurance of *what*?

Maybe I just needed their distraction. I'd gaze at the two eagles gliding the air thermals with such graceful abandon, unconcerned to hunt even. Other birds—waders, crows—are always in an alarmed frenzy when these great raptors approach. They screech warnings or fly behind them as a mob to harass them away, but the eagles are untroubled. Diverted by watching them, I could tolerate being here, perhaps. Here where I was robbed.

But there is a surprise. I am standing on the shore of the lagoon years later now, and don't realize for a while that the two eagles I am watching are a different pair. Their wing feathers are smaller and not black but a dark brown. These are juvenile birds. Vik's eagles have bred, and now there are four.

I've never seen this before. The young eagles are learning to fly. They lunge off from a branch, drift a few moments, then flap back to the nearest tree, urgently. Now they try again, but they tumble. They drop through the air for some moments, almost entangling their wings.

And look. An upside-down eagle. One of the young sea eagles is attempting to dive but is the wrong way around. It's falling on its head, looks like. Legs splayed, talons pointing at the sun, white belly gleaming, head looking up at the sky, not down.

Eight

When it comes to pancakes, my mind goes blank. Try as I might, I can't remember how to make a pancake. I am thrown by this, I who made pancakes so often. Am I so estranged from who I was? The boys ate their pancakes with a syrup of lemon juice and sugar. Steve had his with chicken curry and dhal. And they haven't done this in six years now. I startle myself as I say this. As though it's a new truth, I am stunned. I want to put a fist through these last six years and grab our life. Claim it back.

I want to be in our kitchen late on a Saturday morning as Steve walks in with a paper bag filled with bagels for lunch. I'd toast them with mozzarella, and tomato and basil and chopped green chilies. Steve and I will have a glass of Sancerre. The bagels at our local bakery were nowhere near as good as the ones we bought from the Brick Lane Beigel Bake when the two of us lived in East London long years ago, before the boys were born. We went to late-night movies at the weekends then, and on our way home stopped here for the steaming hot bagels that were pulled from those ovens all night. At three a.m. it was just us and London cabbies cramming into that brightly lit shop where you got a dozen bagels for a pound. We would tell the boys about our lost carefree nights. "It was so good then, we went out all night, and we didn't have you to bother us so we could sleep as late as we wanted on Sundays." They'd look downcast.

In the summer, at weekend lunchtimes, Steve lit up the barbecue. Squid marinated in lemongrass and lime and chili flakes. Slices of salty *haloumi* cheese and lamb chops and sausages from Nicos, our local Greek Cypriot butcher. Nicos always doubted that Steve was English. "The English know nothing about good food, how is he English?" he'd ask, and I'd tell him it was my good influence, and he accepted that.

And often, at the weekends, Steve cooked big meals, and we had friends over. Or his family visited and there would be more than twenty of us for Sunday lunch. He'd make our version of *raan,* an Indian lamb roast. We'd marinate a leg of lamb for two days in a mix of yogurt, almonds, pistachios, lots of spices, mint, and green chilies. Steve watched the roast, concerned that it would not be tender enough, throwing some gin on the meat when basting it. The meat, he'd say, must be so soft, it can be eaten with a spoon.

On quieter days we cooked duck eggs, ate them with crumpets. The boys were impressed by duck eggs. They cupped them in their palms to feel the weight, they tapped the hard shell. Vik would pretend to spin bowl with one, enjoying my agitation as he twisted his fingers around it and lurched forward, raising his arm. He eventually put the egg down, saying, "Calm down, calm down"—in a strange accent (meant to be Liverpudlian). This was something he learned from his father. Regular life. So I thought.

It was at the Sunday farmers' market in Palmers Green that we bought duck eggs. Whenever we went there, Malli would get lost. We usually found him among a heap of purple-sprouting broccoli, his hair sticking up like a baby heron's. We'd buy greengages in August. Often they were perfect, not too yielding, but not unripe. And in the spring Steve bought artichokes. He steamed them with garlic and bay leaves, and we ate them hot. Steve showed the boys how to separate each petal and scrape out the pulp with their bottom teeth. He'd describe to them how he first ate artichokes when he was about ten, and was traveling in his father's lorry somewhere in France.

For my father-in-law, Peter, the isolation of driving a lorry for weeks on end on European roads was redeemed a little by wine and food. Peter shunned the egg and chips served at the truckers' stops. Instead, every evening he coiled his articulated lorry onto narrow country lanes to reach a French or Italian village where he'd made friends with a family who ran a small restaurant, which was usually their dining room, and where each day just one dish was cooked. From the time Steve was about seven, he'd gone with his father on a long trip to Europe during the summer holidays. It was on those journeys that he first tasted risotto, and rabbit stew with bacon, and bouillabaisse, and ravioli that didn't come out of a can, and he loved it all. His friends back home were envious of these trips. But if he began telling them about his culinary adventures, they looked at him blankly and said, "You wha—?" and got on with causing grievous bodily harm to each other playing football, accusing him of "eating foreign." Foreign was not popular fare on an East London council estate in the early 1970s.

But for Steve's family it was. Steve's father was born in Rangoon and lived there and in western India until he came to England with his parents and three brothers in 1946, when he was ten. According to family lore, they were the first Lissenburghs to return to Europe after one Wilhelm Lissenburgh left northern Holland and sailed on a merchant ship to South India in the mid-seventeenth century. When they settled in England, in a small seaside village near Bournemouth, Steve's grandmother and her sisters drove long distances searching for spices and ingredients for making *balachang,* a tangy prawn paste. My mother-in-law, Pam, when she married, quickly learned to eat spicy food and to cook chicken curry. So Steve grew up on curries she made using Bolst's Curry Powder, which came from Bangalore in a tin and which his father relished when he came home at the weekend from Italy or France.

Vik and Malli liked stories about Granddad being a lorry driver and about Steve's travels in the lorry when he was a boy. We'd linger over lunch as Steve described how he slept in a bunk inside the lorry and did his homework as they drove through long tunnels in the Italian Alps. Vik was impressed to learn that Steve even helped Granddad unload his enormous container. Mal was incredulous that sometimes there were only tomatoes in there, so many tomatoes, that's unbelievable. Or rather, unbel*eee*vable, in Malli-speak.

These conversations inevitably ended with Vik complaining about Steve's chosen occupation. He was peeved that Steve had really bungled this. "Why can't *you* be a lorry driver? What's research? I hate research, it's so *boring*, Charlie's dad's a policeman, that's *even* better than being a lorry driver. Isn't it? Isn't it?"

He'd stop grumbling when I gave him his pudding. In the autumn I often made apple-and-blackberry crumble. The two apple trees in our garden go wild with fruit. We sometimes picked blackberries when we went walking in the woods, and Steve instructed the boys to only pick the clusters hanging high in the bushes. "My granddad called the ones lower down pissed-on berries," he would tell them, and they liked that. Later in our oven those urine-free blackberries burst under the crumble and trickled like purple lava across that buttery crust.

In our house, Malee was the best pudding maker. She was much more than a nanny to us, she was our friend. And she spoiled us with her delicious food. She made blueberry muffins with buttermilk and baked bread buns with grated coconut and palm treacle inside. Steve and I returned from work to the warmth of freshly steamed string hoppers and the heady aroma of blackened tuna curry bubbling in a clay pot, thickly spiced and sharp, with lots of *goraka,* a dried, very piquant fruit.

Steve loved cooking seafood. In London we'd get live lobsters from the Wing Yip supermarket off the North Circular Road. I tried not to watch as the man behind the counter took out a couple of live lobsters from a tank and killed them and chopped them and cracked their claws for our stir-fry. In our kitchen that night, chunks of lobster turned crispy in a sauce of black bean, ginger, and shallots and red chili flakes. If the claws were well cracked, the liquid seeped in, and the meat inside was delicious, and Steve helped the boys dig it out with chopsticks. I would tell them that when I was their age and went on holidays in Sri Lanka, my parents bought gunnysacks filled with live crabs from the market, and we'd have crab curry for lunch, very, very spicy.

And that the grown-ups always drank fresh coconut toddy before lunch. And that the toddy smelled like puke, so my cousin Natasha and I sat on the steps of our rented bungalow crying and retching from that stink. The boys were gleeful at the thought of our distress.

Our quest for fish sometimes took Steve and me to Billingsgate Fish Market at dawn. Our friends thought we were quite insane, waking up at four a.m., having Malee sleep over so we could leave home without the children. "Why can't you just go to Waitrose?" they'd ask. The sparkle of big fish markets they just didn't get.

For us it was bliss. We sloshed about from stall to stall on those nippy mornings, drinking coffee that tasted like barely brewed tea, from plastic cups. We'd stop and admire Devon crab in their gleaming purple shells and olive-skinned John Dory with disgruntled deep-sea faces and clawlike spikes on their dorsal fins. We searched for the sea bream with the brightest eyes and flesh that sprang to the touch, and for the plumpest monkfish tails. We bought squid by the boxful, and whole cuttlefish shining in their pinkish cloaks, and tuna, and sometimes swordfish. When we got home, Steve would try to ask Malee nicely if she could clean the squid and cuttlefish, and she would tell him to get lost. If he was mad enough to go out in the wee hours and stink the house out with tons of fish, he could clean it himself. So Steve got further delayed on that report for the Department of Work and Pensions and labored at the kitchen sink, his hands covered in cephalopod slime.

The boys were curious about our early-morning excursions. Did we see a whole swordfish at the market, they'd ask, big sword and all. I had told them that when I was a girl in Sri Lanka, I had a swordfish blade with spikes sticking out of it, I kept it on the bookshelf in my bedroom.

I was about twelve or thirteen when I got that blade. We were holidaying in Wilpattu, a national park in the northwest of the country, and had driven for hours on bumpy dirt tracks to a fishing hamlet deep in the jungle. My parents, uncles, and aunts were in their usual search for lobsters and crabs. The swordfish blade was perched on a broken-down catamaran, and I was looking at it with interest when a very handsome young fisherman came up to me and told me I could have it. Just as I was beginning to enjoy what I thought had been an unnecessary crab-shopping trip, my uncle Bala marched up and asked the young man if he wanted to marry me, boasting my virtues, I always came top in class. The poor boy hurried away, shocked and embarrassed. Someone did take a photo of him, though, bare-chested, wearing a blue and yellow sarong and a shark's tooth tied on a black string around his neck. Some years later I found that photo in a book I'd taken with me when

I went to Cambridge, having failed to make it as a child bride. That photo is still in a box at home in London. I once showed it to the boys. "Much better looking than Dad, no?" I asked. Vik was affronted, "No way!"

I don't want to remember all this. Not alone. I want to fondly reminisce with Steve. It will be one of those days when we've stolen out for lunch. We'll be at La Bota in Crouch End, where the charred baby octopus is so succulent. We didn't get much done on those days we both worked from home. Steve would constantly pop his head around the door of whatever room I was in ("Elevenses?") and we'd sit in the garden and have tea. Or he'd call me into the study ("Remember this?") and play something like that Elvis Costello track he introduced me to in Cambridge. Steve did do a very good Elvis Costello impersonation at the time. That song was "Alison," *Alison* is an anagram for *Sonali*, he told me proudly in his college room, in the days when I didn't take much notice of him. "Hmm," I thought when I first heard those lyrics: "'I heard you let that little friend of mine, take off your party dress.'"

After our wasted days, Steve worked late into the night, two, three a.m. was common. But we always managed an unhurried dinner, just the two of us, once the boys were in bed. I can see Steve now, cooking dhal, a bottle of Chimay in his hand, listening to Coltrane as he watches over the bubbling oil, waiting for the mustard seeds to pop. Eerie but flawless, Steve would say about Coltrane's *Blue Train*. While cooking, he'd leap and dunk a basketball into an imaginary hoop. Come on, play basketball with me, he'd constantly say, and I'd raise my eyebrows and put my feet up on a chair. I was equally impatient when he spoke about his nostalgic love for strawberry-flavored Angel Delight.

I can also feel now the freedom of our Friday nights, when the babysitter came and we headed out. We'd eat at Odette's in Primrose Hill or at Blue Diamond in Chinatown. We'd stop at Bar Italia on Frith Street for double espressos, and we'd take our time sipping them on the pavement outside, even on the coldest nights. Or we'd drive all the way to Green Street in East London, to a Punjabi café that made the best naan bread. Driving around London at night, I loved that, the city felt rightfully ours. True Londoner that he was, Steve understood the city, and I learned it with him. And now, often, when I revisit these places, I am warmed by remembering those easy evenings. But I also often reel. How can there be a London without Steve?

I remember the four of us driving home to North London on our last Sunday in England. We'd been to Fortnum & Mason to buy a Christmas pudding for my mother. Steve wanted to show the boys the new offices his research institute was moving to, near the Post Office Tower. It was raining, and I was in a hurry to get home. "Do it when we're back in January," I said. We'd had lunch at Fortnum's that day, and Vik was thankful that finally we'd brought him to an English restaurant. While Malli considered himself Sri Lankan, Vik insisted he was English, because Daddy was. Steve also bought his favorite Dark Lime Marmalade that day, for when we returned from Colombo.

My friend Anita had cleaned out our kitchen that January, jams and marmalades and all. The first time I went back to our home, I stared at the empty gleaming spice jars in the cupboards, my head in a whirl. Now, each time I am in London, I restock our kitchen, bit by bit. Those white ceramic pots are again filled with turmeric and cloves and cinnamon and fenugreek and flakes of dried fish. But some things in our kitchen I can't bear to even glimpse. I can't touch Steve's oyster knife. I dare not open his cookbooks. It would be too much to see a chili oil stain on a barbecued squid recipe or a trace of a mustard seed on the aubergine curry page of his *Ceylon Daily News Cookery Book*.

Wave

On Steve's very first night in Sri Lanka, he leaped, half-clothed, into the ocean at Galle Face Green at midnight, and I said he was nuts. That was in 1984, when he was nineteen and in his second year at Cambridge and I was in my third. Steve, and our friends Kevin and Jonathan, had come to Colombo with me that summer. They all flung off their shirts that night and dived from the tarred promenade right into those big August waves before I could say anything about the ocean there being dirty or about the strong currents that lurked. We'd only come down to the seafront for a walk, not to swim. Now I had to take them home in the car with their grimy feet and soggy shorts and dripping underpants. Mad, silly boys, I scolded them later, and as always Steve objected to being called a boy, he was a man, and as always then I scoffed.

That first summer Steve played cricket on our street, shirtless and barefoot, with the small boys in my neighborhood. Kevin, Jonathan, and he sat on the high wall at the back of our garden, swigging from large bottles of Lion Lager. They gathered around my father in his library to examine his collection of ancient maps. At dinnertime they stuffed themselves with string hoppers and prawns, Steve's devotion to my mother's prawn curry beginning then. And after dinner I'd leave the door that led

from the balcony to my bedroom unlocked for Steve,
and he'd lie on the double bed he shared downstairs
with Kev, waiting impatiently for my parents to
finally turn in. At the time I still had that ugly painting of a girl playing a violin that someone gave me
for my thirteenth birthday hanging in my room.

They had fifty pounds each, Steve, Kev, and Jonathan, to travel around the country for three months
that summer. Steve sat next to me on the bus, the
elbow he stuck out the window burning in the sun,
and thrilled to the newness of the landscape of the
southern coast. I held my nose as a child threw up
in front. On the beach at Unawatuna, Jonathan
wore a large floppy hat and read a biography of
Lenin under a tree while Kev and Steve flung each
other about in loutish mock fights, chanting, "come
an' have a go if you think you're 'ard enough"—
very childish, I thought. To prove to me they were
capable of more profound emotions, they sang
"Song to the Siren" sitting on a rock, declaring that
when they first heard it played on *John Peel Sessions,*
their hearts stopped.

We went on the train to Nuwara Eliya to spend
a few days with my parents at the Grand Hotel, and
Steve forgot to pack any clothes. How could you
be so stupid, didn't you think your bag was a bit
light, I asked, and when Kev and Jonathan ran out
of clothes to lend him, he wore mine, unconcerned.
Kev took a photo of him swinging from the branch

of a mossy tree on the top of Pidurutalagala Mountain looking ridiculous in my green top.

Four summers after that first trip, Steve arrived in Sri Lanka with a new suit, all his Smiths tapes, and a large carton of duty-free cigarettes for my grandmother, and we got married. We lived in Colombo for the next two years, renting an apartment with an old stone bathtub and overpolished cement floors, and an enormous spider named Insy who hid behind the kitchen sink.

And every night we did averages. We'd sit at the table after dinner, mosquitoes savoring our bare feet. Steve would give me the *Wisden Cricketers' Almanack* and say, "Ask me something." So: "Graeme Hick in 1987?" I'd ask. "Sixty-three point sixty-one," he'd reply. "Viswanath, 1975?" "Eighty-five." "Michael Holding?" "Twenty-three point sixty-eight." "Cowdrey, 1965?" "Seventy-two point forty-four. No, no, seventy-two point forty-one." And so it went. These were batting or bowling averages. He had to (and did) get them correct to the second decimal point. Riveting, married life.

Steve learned the rhythm of my family effortlessly. He joined in the afternoon gossip of my mother and aunts, egging them on with questions about saris and socialites. He bonded with Ma by admiring the rubies on her new earrings and riled her by insisting that her prized silver serving dish looked like the FA Cup. Still, my mother sent him an elaborate lunch every day in a tiffin carrier to the school where he taught economics and played lots of basketball. If his lunch was late, he'd phone my parents' house, but Saroja, our cook, who insisted on calling him *sudu mahattaya* ("white gentleman"), although he pleaded with her not to, would be confused about who was calling until he announced loudly, "This is the white gentleman speaking," leaving the other teachers in the staff room quite aghast. Steve impressed my young cousins with stories from London. His version of Dave and him challenging heavy-booted fascists selling their newspapers on Brick Lane skipped over the bit when the two of them were sent packing and crept into the nearest pub. Steve tried to match my father and uncle in their beer and whiskey drinking but couldn't quite. Da showed Steve the correct way to tie a sarong.

At the temple on full-moon nights Steve patiently held my grandmother by her arm as she took her time distributing coins to rows of beggars who wished her prosperity in her next life. And he smiled even more patiently when she told him, "I really like you, Steve, but I wish Sonali married a nice Sinhala doctor, never mind."

In those first years after we were married, Steve and I traveled around Sri Lanka in a rickety red van he'd borrowed from his school. That van stuttered up the steep road to Horton Plains, and on those chilly grasslands we saw the flashing eyes of hundreds of invisible sambar deer lance the twilight mist. And it was only after he'd inched that van back down a precipitous track that Steve calmly said, "Looks like the brakes are fucked." It was not the brakes that gave up when we slid in the mud on the shores of the Minneriya lake. I bellowed at Steve for not noticing that the van's tires had almost no tread, while near us a serpent eagle split open a fish's gut.

The most frequent trips we made in that red van were to Yala. As a child I spent countless family holidays there, when we stayed for a week in a bungalow in the jungle, and my parents and aunts and uncles always brought too little water and soft drinks for the children but somehow got the quantities for beer right. We'd all sleep, eight beds in a row, on an open veranda at night, with only a three-foot wall between us and an elephant that appeared in the glare of the moon. I loved driving around in a jeep in the dry months when the jungle is a lattice of gray, its monotony broken only by the green burst of a wood apple tree or the red of torn bark. I liked it when the rains came, and the roads were spongy, and the trees instantly turned lime green, and the grass was mosslike in the evening light. While my brother and cousins squabbled over the last drop of Fanta in the back of the jeep, I sat next to my father and learned all about birds.

Now, in the late 1980s, an insurrection in southern Sri Lanka meant hardly anyone came to the

Yala national park. So Steve and I could bask in our solitude, staying weeks at a time in an empty hotel by the sea, where the staff let us get our own beers from the bar because they were too busy playing carom and a tall tusked male elephant with a broken tail roamed outside after dark. It was to become more plush over the years. This was the same hotel we were in when the wave came for us.

Steve was utterly pleased with himself for taking that red van where only a four-wheel-drive jeep should go. We skidded across rocks and struggled in deep sand and nearly toppled over on trails that were mostly washed away. Often we encountered a herd of elephants on a narrow track. We'd park on a side to let them pass, but sometimes they'd tire of us and line up in front of our flimsy red van, coiling trunks, kicking dust, thundering their throats, readying to charge. Steve's hand would reach for the keys to start up the engine, but they would have fallen, and it was only after much fumbling under the seat that we could make our escape. *"Ali madiwata harak,"* Steve would laughingly say about this later, and I'd tease him about his attempt at being clever. He'd picked up some of my mother's countless Sinhala idioms, this one meaning "It's bad enough the elephants are here [to destroy the crops], now the cattle have joined too."

Each evening we'd sip a beer on a rock by the lagoon near our hotel and recount our day's adventures and conjure up our future. As a child, I always wanted to be a ranger in a national park when I grew up, and now Steve's enthusiasm for the wild matched mine. So we canceled our plans to return to England to do Ph.D.'s in economics. We'd become naturalists and live in the jungle, in a tent. Of course we did go back to England and get doctorates in economics. But on those Yala evenings, as the lowering sun gave that lagoon a coating of crushed crimson glass, our dreams made complete sense.

OFF THE MIRISSA COAST, 2011

*T*wo blue whales slip under our boat. I lean over the rails and look. Beneath the sunlit water these whales are blue indeed, an unlikely glowing aquamarine. With a loud rush they surface moments later, dappled gray and startlingly close. We see more whales spouting in the distance—great gusts of mist erupt from the ocean's surface and quickly fade, so fleeting. I count eleven blue whales in all. The two near us don't swim away. They circle our boat, vanishing under it again and again, menacing or playful, who knows. I told my friend Malathi that this boat looked insubstantial when I first saw it at the Mirissa harbor at daybreak. It seems more so now.

But I am too spellbound to be unnerved. I've never seen a blue whale before. I steady myself on this boat that sways in the ocean's swell.

Our boat sits alone in a smoky dark-blue ocean twenty miles from the southern coast of Sri Lanka. There are no other boats in sight, it was some hours ago we last saw land, the sky is bare, no birds. I expand this emptiness, thinking how to the south of us is endless ocean, and then Antarctica. The sea is deep here, it drops two thousand meters to where darkness is complete and some fish have no eyes. Vik knew all about this, the midnight zone.

And Vik was struck by the wonder of blue whales. He grappled with their immensity, as long as three buses, tongue as heavy as an elephant, heart the size of a car, how can that be? He was awed by their ancientness and ancestry. There were whales even sixty million years ago, but isn't it true they looked like dogs? I remembered all this as our boat chugged out of the small harbor. I shouldn't be on this boat, I thought, as I nibbled on a ginger biscuit to stop feeling seasick. Vik never got to see a blue whale. I shouldn't be out searching for whales when Vik can't. It will be agony without him. I'll have hell to pay.

And earlier, as the new heat of day warmed my bench on this wooden boat, their absence crowded me. Up front by the bow, that's where Steve and Vik should be sitting. Malli should be leaning his head on this rail. This sun should be finding the hidden red in his silky black hair. I've flung my flip-flops in that corner, there should be three more pairs piled on top. We always loved the morning ocean, still and soft. The prospect of something this sublime, blue whales, and I couldn't stow away their absence as I sometimes can. It charged out.

The boat entered open ocean, the coastline twisted and tilted behind. This southwest coast we knew so well. I surveyed it now. At the far end of the Mirissa beach, a bright surf lunged at a rocky outcrop, Girigala or "Parrot's Rock," it's called. To the left, the sandy sweep of the Weligama Bay with its waveless, shallow waters and a colorful huddle of fishing boats. And beyond, the octagonal lighthouse at Dondra Head that the British Imperial Light-house Service built in the late nineteenth century. I never tired of telling the boys that this is Sri Lanka's southernmost tip, not that Malli cared when he had a tantrum there because he was hungry and wanted only red bananas. Steve and I planned to have a house along this coast someday soon.

In these six years since they died, I've found it hard to tolerate this landscape. I spurn its paltry picture-postcardness. Those beaches and bays are too pretty and tame to stand up to my pain, to hold it, even a little.

Two silvery flying fish leaped out of the ocean, tails swaying. They wobbled in the air a moment before gliding above the emerald sea, fins trans-formed into gauzy wings. The boat dipped and rolled. We'd been out here for nearly two hours, no hint of whales. The sun was high, lighting fireworks on the water.

Malathi and I talked with Rajesh who navi-gates this boat with a couple of crew. Until recently Rajesh was a fisherman, as were generations of his family before him. Then a few years ago someone discovered that blue whales and sperm whales

migrate along a route in these waters. Now in the
early months of the year when there is no monsoon,
Rajesh does whale-watching trips. He told us about
how he has dived in the presence of blue whales. A
container ship appeared in this otherwise empty
ocean, heading southward. Rajesh instructed us to
hold tight the rail, the ship's passing would make a
big wave, and it did. He steered deftly through it, so
expert, all muscle, quite a lovely scar on his cheek.
Steve should see, how I am impressed.

As the first blow of a whale was sighted, our boat
speeded up, and I was in our living room in London.
Vik and I on the red sofa watching *The Blue Planet*. I
could hear him catch his breath as two blue whales
appear on the screen, impossibly huge even as the
aerial camerawork dwarfs them in an infinite ocean.
He twists his hair faster and faster as they cruise and
dive. And as our boat chopped the water, I wished
the whale ahead of us would disappear. I can't
endure whales without Vik.

But another misty spout beckoned from a few
miles in front, and my want for wild wonder got the
better of me. Blue whales, I was roused. Then that
music from *The Blue Planet* came back to me, the
BBC Concert Orchestra playing that hymnlike blue
whale score. I flinched and bullied my memory. Put
a sock in it, give it a rest.

Now Malathi and I cling to the rails on this open

deck, our eyes transfixed on the two blue whales alongside the boat. We are heady, enthralled. This is the largest creature that has possibly ever lived and, as Malathi tells me, one of the most elusive. Rajesh has turned the boat's engine off. The sea slops against the hull.

It's hard to comprehend a creature of such unearthly dimensions. The two whales rotate around our boat, they move with effortless grace, seeming to have some powerful purpose. The sight of them is staggering, the sensation sacred. I am happy to be here, thankful even.

I want every detail. I want to take in all this blue whale magic, maybe more so because Vik can't. I search the ocean as he would. There is a stir in the water, a foamy mass heralds the head that rises to the surface, its shape an ancient arch. The whale breathes, and a flare of water fizzes in the air. I want to see more now, I want the head to lift higher, that huge pleated jaw, or better still, maybe this whale will breach. But I am left wanting, soon the head is submerged.

They keep their hugeness hidden, these whales, rarely revealing themselves whole to my eager eyes. As one of them cruises underwater, I see burst after burst of glowing blue. When the other breaks surface, the front of its body curves back into the ocean as the rest of it emerges, and the swiftness of this glide gives no hint of hauling impossible bulk. The whales keep their mystery. I am left to infer their might.

The men working on the boat tell us they haven't sighted whales in this sea for some days now. Not since the tsunami in Japan, they say, and they wonder if these creatures were disturbed by it. It is five days now since the earthquake and tsunami hit Japan. And I've not been able to keep away from those television images. As much as they horrify me, I want to see the meanness of that black water as it crumples whole cities in its path. So this is what got us, I thought, when I saw waves leaping over seawalls in Japan. This is what I was churning in. I never saw the scale of it then. This same ocean. Staring at me now all blue and innocent. How it turned.

Where were these whales when the sea came for us? I wonder. Were they in this same ocean? Did they feel a strangeness then? Another whale who was in the distance has come closer now. I hear a loud, low bellow as it exhales. Now the whale inhales. Resounding in this vastness I hear a doleful sigh.

I am hushed. I sit now on a damp cushion on the floor of this boat, not compelled anymore to grab every glimpse of these whales. My earlier discord eases. I don't dread whales without Vik. I don't need so much to duck and dive from remembering. I am unclenched and calmed by the beauty of these creatures, by their pureness, and I savor this relief. Then again I look. This is amazing, now a whale shits. A vast crimson slick slowly fades into the blue water. Ah, you should see this, Vik. All that krill.

I want to stay on this boat forever. I am lulled by the breeze from the sea and the rocking boat. In this endless expanse of ocean, I feel snug. These blue whales are unreal and baffling, yet surrounded by them I settle awhile. Somehow on this boat I can rest with my disbelief about what happened, and with the impossible truth of my loss, which I have to compress often and misshape, just so I can bear it— so I can cook or teach or floss my teeth. Maybe the majesty of these creatures loosens my heart so I can hold it whole. Or have I been put in a trance by these otherworldly blue whales?

It feels as though I am in a dream here, in this slow haze of sea and sky. A whale now dives. For the first time I see the great flukes of a blue whale tail rise out of the water. The dive takes just moments, but for me this time slowly unfurls. The water sliding off that lifted tail seems to freeze into stalactites.

And I remember now another dream. Some months after the wave, Anita told me about a dream Kristiana had. She was eight years old then, bewildered by the loss of her friends. One morning at breakfast, Kristiana insisted that Vik and Malli had come back home. She talked about her dream of the previous night. She saw Vik and Mal, they were holding hands, they were walking out of the sea.

Wave

The tail of the diving whale slaps down and
vanishes into the blue. This is a deep dive, the whale
has left us. I see the glassy imprint of its tail tremble
on the water, but soon it smooths away. The ocean
is losing its morning stillness. It's gone noon, waves
gather, the boat shudders.

We head back to shore, and I tell Malathi that blue
whales and Steve and I go back a long way. There
was an early story that Steve told me. It made me
notice him as more than an always-drunk eighteen-
year-old from East London who'd made it to
Cambridge. He'd described to me an experience he
had on his first visit to the Natural History Museum
when he was six years old. It was a school trip. He
walked into the Blue Whale Gallery not knowing
what was awaiting him. Then he saw the life-size
model of a blue whale. The intensity of feeling that
arose in him made tears stream from his eyes, he
said. He was utterly overwhelmed, this was the
most stirred he'd ever been. He'd never suspected
such magnificence could exist. He was a little boy
who'd rarely ventured outside the block of council
flats he lived in, and now this sight, an epiphany.
But he was also fearful. He knew he'd be tormented
by his friends if they saw even a hint of his tears. In
his inner-city school, even if you were only six, you
couldn't cry about whales.

*B*efore I left Colombo for Cambridge at the age of eighteen, my mother fussed about the bland English food I'd have to eat and tried to teach me to cook dhal. But onions made me nervous. I'd been this way since I was three, when my aunts locked me in the onion room in my grandmother's house—to punish me for disturbing their afternoon siesta, most likely. That shadowy room was scattered with wicker baskets swarming with small red onions. From that day I hadn't been able to touch an onion or eat it raw—an onion peel drifting somewhere in the house, and I'd call for someone to clear it away. Apart from onions I wasn't anxious about anything when I went to university. I was leaving Sri Lanka for the first time, I'd never lived away from my family, and I was parting from all my friends in the girls' school I'd been to since I was four. But I was unperturbed. Everything that mattered then—studying, making friends, flirting—came easily to me, and I was cheerily secure. But Aaththa, my grandmother, worried for me. Every evening, after scolding the servants for bruising the jasmines they'd picked for her, she would light an oil lamp and offer the ruined flowers to a stone Buddha and pray that I wouldn't marry an *ali wandura*—an "albino monkey," aka a white man.

During my first winter in Cambridge in 1981, it

snowed so heavily that my self-assurance crumpled. I regarded the icy mess that was the Huntingdon Road in dismay—to get to lectures, I have to cycle two miles on *that*? My new friends were patient. Their bikes flanked mine on either side and back and front as I teetered along. We quickly became a close-knit group, those of us who read economics at Girton, spending most of our waking hours together, moving in a pack. When I first met David and Alan, they announced to me that they'd come to Cambridge for "excellence, excellence, excellence," but a few months later, David was skipping lectures with me so we could listen to *Our Tune* on Radio One. Lester, who was a year above us, would sometimes try to hide his East London heritage during Formal Hall by pretending, unsuccessfully, that he was a Nigerian prince. Clive impressed us all, he'd had a gap year and gone busking with his fiddle in Mexico. Seok, who was from Singapore, and I were the foreigners. Not only was she more skilled on a bicycle than I was, she wore punk makeup and Goth clothes. I wore a bright blue Michelin Man–looking jacket given to me by my aunt.

In that first year I had a lot to learn. Grasping Keynesian critiques of monetarism was the relatively easy part. I struggled more with *Life of Brian,* my first Monty Python film. I didn't get half the jokes. I persuaded myself to like The Clash just because David did, I bought *Combat Rock.* My friends and I were heady with our recent initiation into left-wing politics, hardly taking time to sleep for discussing the crises of capitalism. To protest against Thatcherite policies of cutting public spending at a time of high unemployment, in the Cambridge Union I sat next to a young man wearing polka-dot trousers and threw eggs at Sir Geoffrey Howe.

I'd been in Cambridge a year when Steve arrived. He'd also came to Girton to read economics.

"Does it rain here often?" This was the first thing Steve said to me. Except he said "rhine," not rain, and I stared at him thinking, *What?* He was standing behind me in the lunch queue, a tall and skinny eighteen-year-old, with a wooden tray in his hand. He repeated his question in response to my blank look, scarlet-cheeked now. When I figured out what he'd said, I still thought, *What?* I gave some uninterested reply and turned to the curly-haired boy who was with him—Kevin, he told me his name was— hoping for a more inspiring chat. Steve later told me he thought then, you arrogant cow.

Steve and Kevin relied on each other to navigate Cambridge, an untried terrain for these two working-class boys, Steve from East London and Kevin from Basildon in Essex. So at the sherry reception to meet the Mistress of the college, Steve nudged Kevin as he told her, "Me and me friend want to . . ." but too late, she corrected him and said "You mean, my friend and I." Kev tried to stop

Steve picking out and eating the leaves from the cup of green tea he'd been served by their economic history professor during a tutorial—"No, mate, you don't do that, no." In those days Steve wore a green bomber jacket, Doc Martens boots, and a West Ham football scarf. This look of urban toughness was at once defeated because his grandmother had knitted STEPHEN across his scarf, as you would for a five-year-old.

The two of them quickly became the comics in our group. They regaled us with wildly exaggerated impersonations of characters from their local neighborhoods, savoring the knowing that in Cambridge they would not be maimed for this, as they would be back home. So they'd act the thief who stole his neighbor's TV and displayed it in his own living room—even though the neighbor was a friend who often popped over for a chat (and probably to watch *Crimewatch UK,* who knows). Or "hard men" who strutted the streets saying, "You lookin a' me or chewin' a brick?" and were affronted if you looked them in the eye. And those with ambitions to make it big in the world of crime—wannabe bank robbers and bare-knuckle fighters who lived by the code of not "grassing up" friend or foe to the law. This was the first I'd heard of Cockney rhyming slang and learned that *tea leaf* was "thief" and *butcher's hook* meant "look" and *trouble and strife* was, of course, "wife."

Every evening Steve and Kevin were drunk, vomit arcing over Trinity Bridge or dripping down shut windows that hadn't been opened fast enough. I kept my distance. "Her ladyship," they'd tease me. "Look, she's miffed, she's turning her nose up at us." Two rowdy boys, I thought, not yet fully formed.

So I wasn't seeking Steve's interest when each morning I sauntered down the hallway we shared wearing a transparent white kurta and no underwear—I'd only just woken up and was going to the bathroom. But this encouraged him to come to my room with his copy of *The Complete Poems of John Keats* and read from it. That book was stained with black grease, he'd taken it with him on his travels across Europe in his father's lorry the previous summer. He told me he read Keats's "Lamia" sitting on a crate in a warehouse in Milan, and not even the din of unloading trucks could distract him from Lamia the serpent transforming herself into a woman, writhing and foaming—"her elfin blood in madness ran." Now from "Lamia" he read me the lines "Eclipsed her crescents, and licked up her stars" several times over. You *could* be a tad more subtle, I thought.

But he had glossy black hair that fell across his forehead and very distinct, slanted dark eyes and a pointy chin. Sweet. So I enjoyed the occasional hours we had together, just the two of us, without Kevin or the rest of our friends. We went for long walks on a dirt track by fields where the veterinary science department kept deviant-looking bulls with oddly shaped heads. And through St. John's playing fields at dusk. I was still unaccustomed to how early daylight caved in on English autumn afternoons. We hurried to the tearoom of University Library when the hot scones were served. I was bored with the economics I had to study that year and readily gave up grappling with Sraffa's theory of value to linger with Steve among the stacks in the North Wing, reading pamphlets on party games in the British colonies or books on East End villains like the Kray twins. Steve told me that not too far from where he lived, in Whitechapel, was the Blind Beggar Pub where the Krays shot someone.

Steve was full of stories about his family and his childhood and about the London he knew. He'd grown up in Manor Park, on the outer edges of East London—"growing up on the Manor," it was called locally. It was here that Steve played football with his brother, Mark, late into the night under streetlamps. He loitered with his friends outside the sweet factory nearby, imagining the rich pickings inside. They ate tomatoes that grew wild by the sewage works near the Roding River, a trifling tributary of the Thames, and their faces broke into a rash. One day Steve's father told him that he'd smash his kneecaps if he saw him hanging around too many street corners. Steve knew his dad wouldn't but was thankful for the threat. It allowed him to stay in and do his homework when his friends called round, yet again, to go hurl milk bottles against the wall of the social club at the end of their street. "Na, not tonight, mate, me dad'll kill me."

His father's long absences from home due to his job meant that Pam, his mother, raised Steve, his brother, and his two sisters largely on her own. She did so cheerfully and very volubly. When Steve was little, she'd embarrass him no end by bemoaning to everyone at the launderette the fact that his ears stuck out, as the two of them folded the family laundry. Although Pam's daily life was confined to their East London neighborhood, she had a great curiosity about world affairs and politics. And of all her children, it was Steve who paid attention to her interests. As a teenager, he'd spend long evenings lying on the sofa with his head on his mother's lap, evaluating for her the French parliamentary system or explaining the Spanish transition to democracy. His mother's other passion was romance novels—she read one a night—and Steve and his sister Jane would be instructed to buy secondhand paperbacks by the dozen for her from a stall in Green Street Market.

They'd stop by the market on their way to see West Ham play at Upton Park on Saturdays. Since Steve was about seven, Jane, who was five years older, took him to football matches. After the game they'd visit their grandmother, who lived near the stadium in a flat full of clutter above a Chinese takeaway. She always told Steve he was bright because he took after her sister, who was "the cleverest woman in Rangoon." In Rangoon, his grandmother's father was the supervisor of a slaughterhouse, and she spent her days playing tennis or going to garden parties.

His details caught my fancy—so many yarns, tender and funny. My stories of my childhood seemed meager in comparison. I told him about my first trip to the cinema when I was five, to see *My Fair Lady*. My parents had to bring me home halfway because I began howling at the steaming hot bath that was being run for Eliza. We had only cold showers then in Sri Lanka, and I thought she was about to be boiled alive. This upset me more than the stilt walker who came down our street once a week in the afternoons, when my mother was having a nap and I was playing outside.

Despite that early nervous talk about rain, Steve had a self-belief that ran deep, I soon learned. He was unruffled, at ease with himself. When we had exams or essays to write, he had remarkable focus. He worked intently, nimble and efficient in identifying what was important from those absurdly vast reading lists. Always precise, those notes he scribbled with a pencil on revision cards in the hush of the library's Manuscript Room.

Steve came to Cambridge from a secondary

school that was academically dismal. When they were sixteen, a couple of his peers would spell Hitler as "Itla." The street outside was lined with police riot vans at the end of the school day. Mobs of students who played truant turned up at the gates to fight others who'd spent the day wrecking classrooms. Apart from our friend Lester, who'd been to that same school, no one went to university, some went to prison. On hearing that Steve was off to Cambridge, one of the veteran delinquents assumed it was just another borstal and said, "Which one's that then? What's the grub like there?"

Steve was always relaxed about the bedlam in his secondary school. It even worked to his advantage, he told me. For he had the undivided attention of his teachers, a rare student they could actually teach, and he thrived. And the troublemakers let him. He had respect for being on the basketball team. It also pleased a few of his white peers that "one of them" was excelling. "That'll show the Pakis," they'd say, perceiving that it was mainly Asians who achieved anything academically in that school. This was the late 1970s and early 1980s, when notions of white supremacy were widespread among groups of youth in deprived neighborhoods. The distress he felt about the prejudice and hatred around him, Steve poured into his troubled teenage poems about the corrupt urban soul.

Some Sunday afternoons in Cambridge, the two

of us would go study in a meadow or an orchard, a bottle of Southern Comfort in hand. The English countryside had no allure for me as yet, and I would complain that it was boring, no wild elephants charging at us. Steve declared that, unlike me, he could find charm in any landscape. He described how he'd luxuriate in the glow of early sunlight striking red brick on his council estate as he cycled through its streets every morning delivering newspapers for Patel's, the newsagents on Romford Road.

We would hitchhike from Cambridge to London a few times a term, the group of us. We'd go to the Reading Room in the British Library and to Highgate Cemetery, out of reverence for Karl Marx. Our friend Seok introduced us to Cantonese roast duck and rice at Kai Kee on Wardour Street. It was on one of these trips that Steve's great passion for the bronze Sri Lankan statue of the goddess Tara in the British Museum was ignited. Another time, one December afternoon, he made Seok and me walk around his neighborhood for hours looking for the place he buried his Action Man when he was six. It was cold and dull—what was that nonsense he'd told me about radiant red brick?—and I was pouting.

But the next morning when Steve came to my room and sat on my bed, I reached for him. To save him the bother of, yet again, reading Keats. He was very eager, of course, so sweetly intense, but before long he said, "Back in a minute," and left. I later learned this pause was so he could sprint to Kevin's room and bang on his door and brag "I snogged Sonal" and relish his friend's response. Kev threw him onto the floor. "You lucky bastard, you jammy git." Had I known then of this silliness over a kiss, I would never have let him in my room again that cold December morning. But he came bounding back. And stayed a good while.

Nine

I am not one for telling. So it might be the
mojitos that make me confess. I had two with
dinner. No, I think, three. The night was clear, and
the ocean quiet. Even in the dark I could see pelicans
dive.

These are perilous days, my boys' birthdays. They
make me anxious as they approach. In these past six
years I've spent this time with friends. We traveled to
new landscapes, some of them vast and fierce, they
echoed my tumult, some diverted me, a little. There
was a blizzard on a glacier in Iceland and a storm
that rocked our car by a lonely Scottish loch. We got
tangled in pondweed swimming in the Berkshires,
in Madrid we sought out the bars.

Now this time it's different. It was Vikram's
birthday two days ago, and again I traveled. But
alone. I wanted an unfamiliar vista to help me
endure the day, and I was curious—do I dare spend
this time on my own? When I came to Miami from
New York, I told myself, it's not far, if I am too

wrecked, I can always come back. Vik would have been fourteen two days ago. Fourteen.

I didn't at first trust the lightness I felt. It's just Miami, all this gaiety around me, I am getting carried away, I am being duped into feeling nothing is amiss, I thought. How could I be this comfortable otherwise? Yet my ease didn't fade. Each day I walked on the beach in the early sun, the wind was wild, and I felt brisk and fresh. I dipped in the ocean, time and again, let the salt sting my arms. There was a downpour last night, and I swam in an empty pool, spring rain cutting my face. I was peaceful in that water, I found a brightness in myself I didn't think I now possessed.

This was a discovery. On days like this, birthdays, the anniversary of the wave, I want to be alone. Alone, I am close to them, I slip back into our life, or they slip into mine, undisturbed.

The young bartender at this hotel is a student. He has lots of questions when I tell him I am an academic, in London, now at Columbia. I give advice where I can but keep it brief. I am guarded when conversations with strangers go on too long—questions about family might arise. So each evening the young man fixes my third excellent mojito and says with a broad smile, "Professor on spring break." I think, if only you knew, sweetheart.

It still seems far-fetched, my story, even to me. Everyone vanishing in an instant, me spinning out from that mud, what is this, some kind of myth? Even now I cannot mouth those words "They are all dead." So at best I am vague about family. At other times I lie and find myself in a pickle. "Are your parents well?" a neighbor in my building in New York will ask if I have just returned from Colombo, because previously she has asked whether my parents live in Sri Lanka and I have mumbled, "Yes."

The Rosenbaums looked about my parents' age, dressed smartly for dinner as my parents would have done, maybe that's why I started chatting to them. They are here for the weekend too, in Miami, at the Standard Hotel. I said something innocuous like "Nice here, isn't it?" when he said hello. "Oh, I don't know about that," he promptly replied. "I feel very out of place." I was only being polite, but now I couldn't just walk away.

Turns out it was very different forty years ago, this hotel. That was when his parents spent entire winters here, with their friends, lots of Jewish retirees. His wife and he came back today for the memories. And to celebrate their wedding anniversary. But he didn't expect *this,* a boutique hotel, swarming with young people, barely clothed. He feels extremely awkward among them, what at his age?

More than an hour later, we are still in conversation. "And another thing," he says each time I stand up to leave, and his wife smiles at me in apology. "I'm sure she wants to go to her room, dear," she keeps telling him, but he takes no notice. He is curious. How do I find it, traveling alone like this? I say, fine. He is persistent in seeking my opinions. So I am from London, did Turner live his entire life by the Thames, walking by the riverside? As an economist, what do I think of the Great Recession, the stimulus package, the euro, how do I explain the economic success of the Jews? And he disagrees, at great length, with all my answers.

This I find endearing. Familiar also. In Sri Lanka I know lots of contrarian characters like him, uncles, fathers of friends, charming for all their rants and their grouchiness. What a smart, cheerful young woman you are, he keeps remarking. (I assure him I am not young, but that he ignores.) He is so enjoying our chat, he feels he knows me well, I must promise to keep in touch. It's turning chilly out here now, I bid goodnight, again. He kisses me on both cheeks and says, "I don't know what's wrong with young men these days, a lovely young woman like you, you shouldn't be single." I don't respond. He must think he's made some blunder. "Oh, oh, have you ever been married?" he asks. I would normally have said no and left.

But the drinks have made me mellow, and I have this new ease, and that makes me honest, so I say, "Yes." "Was your husband English?" "He was." "Aah, that was the problem, you see. You should have married a nice Jewish boy, this would never have happened." I pause for a moment, then understand. The *this* is me being dumped by some useless English scoundrel.

Hang on. I am really not one for telling. But I must defend Steve. "It's *not* because he is *not Jewish*," I blurt out without thinking. "It's because he is *dead*." What have I just said? I stun myself with my own words. *Dead?* My new friend looks so sorry, the poor man. And he doesn't even know the half of it.

Wave

I trip up constantly, between this life and that. Even now, seven years on. A rush of footsteps in the apartment above me is all it takes. It brings me at once into our home in London. I think it's the boys, upstairs, another scuffle. "Knock it off," I almost shout. "I'm trying to, Mum," I hear Vik, ribbing me, as he aims a ball at his brother's head. Then I have to accept that I don't have them. I am in New York.

But our banter doesn't subside in me. This is very different from those early months after the wave, when all I heard was a sudden whisper, some snatches of sound. Their voices have doubled in strength now, not faded with time. Their chatter plays with my thoughts no end. And I am sustained by this, it gives me spark. I often think I utter Steve's words, not mine. Or at least that's my excuse.

It used to startle me. The sudden realization of not having them, of being alone here in New York. I'd find myself gasping violently as I stood outside my apartment building in the West Village. I am here because they are *gone*? That was when their absence, as well as their realness, was wavering and suspect. It's different now. I know it is true that they are not here. An unfathomable truth, but maybe I am more accustomed to it.

New York has given me the distance from which I can reach for my family. From here I travel back and forth to London and Colombo, rediscovering us. And I can absorb my findings free from the fear of always colliding with the too familiar—the milkman, a Sainsbury's wine gum wrapper, Camden Town. When I first came to this city, I would wander along Doyers Street with its quiet row of barbershops that seem from a bygone age, and my mind would slowly unclench, and allow in glimpses of us.

Last evening I walked downtown along the Hudson at sunset, as I often do. I stopped on the boardwalk on Pier 46 to watch the orange light. There was a canopy of hysterical gulls over my head, the birds were spinning and swerving, no end to their agitation, it seemed. And standing there, I could enter another vista, see another river. The four of us on a Saturday afternoon at Butler's Wharf, by the Thames. I am impatient, shooing along the boys who are dillydallying in the drizzle because they think Tower Bridge is about to open, any minute now. I could hear it, the chords of my sons' protests, Steve's elected silence, much better to let me be the spoiler of all fun.

Wave

More and more now I keep my balance while staring into us. And I welcome this, a small triumph, it lights me up.

But of course, it also shifts, this equilibrium. This morning I sip my coffee on a bench in St. Luke's Garden in the West Village, where the early summer light froths on the hydrangeas and foxgloves. Such an English garden, this. I notice the whiff of a dead insect on my fingers, one of those tiny mites that skid the air and become a smudge on your hand as you wave it away. This transports me instantly to our garden in London which teems with these midges in warmer months. And I see us, idling after breakfast on the patio on a Sunday morning. I pester Steve to massage my neck. I hear Vik, with deepening voice, now fifteen. Then I lurch into what I am missing.

I am immersed in another reality. Our life, as it would be today. When I've trespassed here through the years, I've kept my projections imprecise. But lately the details of how we would now be have come striding in, lucid, quite exact. My alertness to the "us now" is so immediate, it's as though I've only just been torn from our life.

I know it intimately. My world, if I had them. The rip, the clamor, the colors, the milestones, the odors, two teenage boys.

This is treacherous, my alertness to what will never be. I want to stifle it, somehow.

Seven years on, and their absence has expanded. Just as our life would have in this time, it has swelled. So this is a new sadness, I think. For I want them as they would be now. I want to be in our life. Seven years on, it is distilled, my loss. For I am not whirling anymore, I am no longer cradled by shock.

And I fear. Is this truth now too potent for me to hold? If I keep it close, will I tumble? At times I don't know.

But I have learned that I can only recover myself when I keep them near. If I distance myself from them, and their absence, I am fractured. I am left feeling I've blundered into a stranger's life.

I am also split off from myself when I don't reveal. It's like I'm in a witness protection scheme, I've often thought of my life in New York. I needed this, a cover-up, when I was stunned. But it is different now. I suspect that I can only stay steady as I traverse this world that's empty of my family when I admit the reality of them, and me.

For I am without them, as much as I am on my own.

And when I hold back this truth, I am cut loose, adrift, hazy about my identity. Who am I now?

There was a thunderstorm last night, so this

garden is perky, and my bench is wet. I see damp mornings on our lawn in London, Malli picking a dandelion, sticking it in my hair.

And now I remember. How Malli would describe and define me. And how I'd protest.

"We are three boys and one girl, three boys and one girl," he'd say, explaining his family, working out our composition as he hopped across the paving stones on the patio. Then he'd recite our names, even referring to himself as Nikhil, his given name, and not Malli, as he was always called. "Stephen Lissenburgh, Vikram Lissenburgh, Nikhil Lissenburgh, and Mummy Lissenburgh." He'd announce us with aplomb.

Mummy Lissenburgh? I'd roar in exaggerated objection. My new credentials. Me having no identity without these three boys to whom I was merely tagged on. "Malli, why do you get *both* my names wrong? You got everyone else's right. *That's* not me."

Steve enjoyed our son's account of me, of course. He egged him on. "Clever boy, Mal, spot on, you're exactly right. *You* tell it like it is." So "Mummy Lissenburgh!" Malli would chant. And the three silly boys would fall about laughing. Now I sit in this garden in New York, and I hear them, jubilant, gleeful, on our lawn.

Acknowledgments

Thank you most of all to Mark Epstein, my extraordinary therapist. This book would not exist without his guidance and persuasion. With him I was safe, to try to grasp the unfathomable, and to dare to remember.

A huge thank-you to Radhika Coomaraswamy, Sarah Gordon, Malathi de Alwis, and Amrita Pieris, who read every fragment of this book, and kept insisting on more, through the years.

Many thanks to Swyrie and Ken Balendra, Beverley Wood, Naomi Collett, Anita Grigoriadis, Margaret Headland, Natasha Balendra, Ruvanthi Sivapragasam, Carole Burgher, Kevin Brown, Lester Hudson, Maria Hudson, Sithie Tiruchelvam, David Brown, Keshini Soysa, Linda Spalding, Suki Sandler, and Sophie Wood, who responded to the book and encouraged me at various stages of writing.

My profound thanks to Michael Ondaatje, whose support has meant so much to me.

I am truly grateful to my agent, Ellen Levine. Many thanks to Lennie Goodings.

Acknowledgments

Many thanks to Carol Devine Carson, Pei Loi Koay, and Gabrielle Brooks at Knopf, and to Kendra Ward and Scott Richardson at McClelland and Stewart.

A very special thank-you to Sonny Mehta and Diana Coglianese in New York, and to Ellen Seligman, in Toronto. I am so moved by all they have done to bring this book into the world. Their care and dedication as my publishers and editors have been phenomenal, and it's been such a treat to work with them.